FOOD FROM THE FAMILY TREE

Bygone Days
Meet Modern Ways

Patricia J. Bell
Bonnie J. Rasmussen

moreland
mp
PUBLISHING

Happy reading, cooking & eating!

B J Rasmussen

FOOD FROM THE FAMILY TREE is published by Moreland Publishing, P.O. Box 416, Wrightsville Beach, North Carolina 28480.

Text and Illustrations Copyright © 2008 by Patricia J. Bell and Bonnie J. Rasmussen

Design and layout by Moreland Publishing
Cover Design by Matt Baumgardner

Library of Congress Control Number
2001012345

ISBN 10: 0-9796833-1-9
ISBN 13: 978-0-9796833-1-2

Printed in the United States

To
Sophie and Helen

"All new dishes fade,
The newest oft the fleetest,
Of all cakes ever made,
My Mother's still the sweetest"
....Anonymous

ACKNOWLEDGMENTS

FOR THEIR ESSENTIAL CONTRIBUTIONS IN HELPING TO MAKE
THIS BOOK HAPPEN, OUR HEARTFELT THANKS GO TO THE
FOLLOWING—IN ORDER OF THEIR APPEARANCE:

Mary Beth, gifted culinarian, with whom the dream of ever doing a book of any
kind was first hatched—Joyce, chief muse and source of support without whom
this book would never have been finished—Matt, master of software mysteries—
Doranda, trusted tester and taster—countless friends who offered their tasting
services—Shirley, writing cheerleader with an unerring artistic eye—Elaine, editor
supreme and kindest critic—Jeff, who generously shared his printing expertise—

AND
OF COURSE

Special thanks to stalwart spouses:
Bill and Wes

TABLE OF CONTENTS

PREFACE - Pandora's Box

We weren't planning to write this book. It wasn't even a blip on the radar screen of things we thought we might do someday. The idea just crept up on us. It was the end of a long day spent emptying Mother's house, dust and dirt covered our jeans and tee shirts, and we were exhausted. Sitting cross-legged on the floor—there was nothing else left to sit on—we eyed the dilapidated cardboard carton into which we had dumped the contents of the last kitchen drawer yet to be sorted before we could call it quits. It was that catchall drawer, which every kitchen seems to have, holding a maybe-we'll-need collection of old corks, rubber bands, twist ties, a ball of twine, leftover birthday candles, pencil stubs, rusty scissors, and the like. We were seized by the impulse to just chuck the lot, but, owing to some tiresome genes passed down from Mother and Grandma, we were too obsessively responsible not to sift through the stuff.

Looking for something worth salvaging, we came upon Mother's battered wooden recipe box. It was crammed so full with food-spotted, handwritten index cards and yellowed recipe clippings that the lid stayed shut only with the aid of a fat purple rubber band. Recorded on assorted bits of paper were the dishes our mother and her mother routinely prepared during our growing-up years: buttermilk biscuits, rice pudding, gingerbread, tuna casserole, lemon bar cookies, smothered pork chops….Each recipe held memories of the simple comfort of everyday homey meals, family togetherness, and the fellowship of friends gathered round the table. The dishes were among of the first things we learned to cook under Mother's watchful eye.

Wistfully we thought how dated all those dishes looked now, how dowdy when stacked up against today's cosmopolitan cuisine. Over the years, the stay-at-home mom making oatmeal bread from scratch had gone from endangered species to virtual extinction. We too had moved away from this food, seduced by the latest culinary trend or diet to hit the market. The old-fashioned dishes of our childhood had gradually been transformed in our hands: infused with international flavors, enlivened with "exotic" ingredients from today's multicultural marketplace, streamlined with shortcut techniques to accommodate time-crunched work schedules, and slimmed down for today's more sedentary life styles and health consciousness.

In Mother's later years, as she battled breast cancer, we took over cooking for her, preparing our interpretations and variations on the dishes she had made for us as children. Though we had never really thought much about it, we were struck by how important food is as a bench-mark of changing times in general as well as a mirror of our individual journeys from past to present. Home cooking is a link between generations, and, as an ongoing evolutionary source of comfort and nurturing for both body and spirit, it reflects the true meaning of family.

In the gathering darkness we packed up the recipe box and, without a twinge of guilt, threw out everything else in the carton. We had the important stuff...and a sudden conviction that we had to do something with it.

INTRODUCTION

This book is about three generations of women and their cooking. Practically speaking, it is a collection of homey, uncomplicated, guaranteed-to-please dishes that we prepare on an everyday basis—and you can too with a minimum of time and effort. But, in a larger sense, the book is about food and family. Although we make many of the same things that our mother and her mother did, the resulting dishes often differ markedly from their antecedents, reflecting the raw materials available and climate of the times, as well as the individuals' life styles and taste preferences. The recipes represent a new style of eating based on an international marketplace of ingredients, increased health consciousness, time- and labor-saving considerations, and a make-ahead stockpiling philosophy that promotes a time-shifting way to cook. Despite the obvious differences, the dishes that we make can trace their culinary ancestry back to Grandma and Mother's cooking in spirit as well as basic components. Chronicling their evolution from past to present, we hope to show how the old-time comfort of home-cooked family meals we all yearn for at some level can be achieved within the context of today's pressured living.

THE LEGACY

We are essentially a clan of females. The offspring in our immediate family have all been girls, and a matriarchal line has dominated the kitchen turf. Although there is the necessity of feeding a family, we cook primarily because it is something we love to do. Time flies by when we are in the kitchen, a room that has always ended up being the central gathering place in our houses. And, even though cooking has its drudge aspects—who's going to do the dishes?—food and its preparation hold a fascination that seems to be in our genes. Carrying on a tradition from our grandmother and mother, we enjoy feeding others and welcoming them into our homes for a meal, whether it be a celebration or just a simple neighborly get together. We find that food is a way of comforting and nurturing on a personal level as well as fostering fellowship and camaraderie.

Grandma represented the first branch of our family tree to establish itself on American soil. Although her roots were Austrian, her cooking reflected the era in which she lived and her particular life circumstances as much as her geographical or cultural heritage. As children, we were sure Grandma was the best cook on the planet. Her house always smelled wonderful—full of the aromas of fresh garden flowers and enticing food—and meals at Grandma's were great spreads of delicious homey dishes. From today's perspective the miracle was how she managed to pull all this off considering what she had to work with. Produce was often basic and locally limited, and milk and ice were still delivered daily. Having raised a daughter through depression and war years, Grandma had a backyard Victory Garden and canned, pickled, and preserved summer's bounty to guard against leaner times. Extra vegetables and preserves were swapped for eggs from neighbors who had chickens. Grandma never learned to drive, so each morning

Grandpa took her into town in the old Packard, to the butcher shop and grocer and fishmonger while he visited with his cronies at the post office and barber shop. Everything Grandma put on the table was cooked "from scratch." Her kitchen itself bore a strong resemblance to rooms we might now see in a museum's olden-days diorama, and the crockery along with many of the utensils she used are now decorative collectibles in our own kitchens. Grandma never owned a cookbook, and the few recipes she wrote down contained instructions such as "add butter the size of an egg." She rarely measured, trusting instead on a look, feel, and taste approach. Nothing in her vast culinary repertoire would likely qualify as haute cuisine in today's terms, but the secret ingredient of loving care gave everything a matchless flavor and goodness.

Mother learned to cook the way all young girls of her era did—watching and helping her mother in the kitchen. A newly minted college nursing school graduate, she soon became a WWII army bride and young mother. With the arrival of peacetime her generation of home-makers saw vast changes in the culinary landscape including supermarket shelves piled high with new-fangled things like margarine, frozen foods, tin-canned goods, and various processed foods and mixes. In addition to preparing family meals, Mother cooked for such things as covered-dish supper get togethers, bake sales, children's birthday celebrations, and chafing-dish cocktail parties. Her kitchen in the little house where we grew up was not large to begin with. Then there were those five doorways: to the dining room, living room, pantry, cellar, and back porch. Chockablock in the room were a huge pilot-lighted gas cookstove, a cumbersome wringer washing machine, a sink/drainboard combo, one tiny drawer unit with an enameled metal top, a quaint old radiator, and—sardined-in under a window—a booth-like breakfast table with benches. The refrigerator (a step up from Grandma's icebox) was crammed into the minuscule pantry, along with all the pots and pans and basic provisions. There wasn't one storage cabinet in the entire place. And countertop? An island? Such extravagances were beyond Mother's realistic, practical dreams. In these modest and cramped quarters we learned to make cookies as well as master a few other culinary basics that Mother felt would one day help us find husbands and keep them from starving. It was here too that our love of cooking got its start and some of our most lasting food memories were formed.

Between us we have designed or remodeled five kitchens. Bonnie is putting the finishing touches on a sixth in her new mountain North Carolina aerie, and a seventh is on the drawing board for Pat's house, under construction in coastal North Carolina. The custom cabinetry, stainless steel equipment, granite counters, programmable appliances, and labor-saving tools that we take for granted today would be as unimaginable as space travel was to Grandma. Our kitchens now buzz and hum with the advent of disposals, compactors, convection ovens, micro-waves, and an assemblage of electronic gadgetry designed to accomplish more efficiently virtu-ally everything that was once done by hand. Foreign travel is now commonplace, ethnic restau-rants have become mainstream, and formerly exotic produce has widespread availability. These factors, combined with the hectic schedules of working mothers and the activity-filled, technol-ogy-addicted lives of children, have altered the pattern of family life in general and changed our dining habits dramatically. It certainly has changed the way we regard food. We like to think that we plan healthy creative menus using a variety of cooking techniques and a broad range of ingredients. Seldom does a week go by that we don't eat Chinese, Thai, Mexican, Italian, or Indian. Multicultural and melting pot fusion—it's now the American way in a world far smaller than it was generations ago. We want to eat interesting, healthy food, but we also want meal preparation to be as easy and efficient as possible.

Though we might not want to return to the "good old days," a growing discontent with an entrenched fast-food culture and consequent rash of obesity has spawned a grass roots move to feed ourselves and our children better. Building on the legacy of home-cooking of our child-hood, the recipes in this book represent a way to do just that. Through the anecdotes that introduce each recipe, you will meet us, our mother, and our grandmother. We will share with you some of our favorite everyday dishes, their origins and their evolution. International and multicultural flavor variations are included along with shortcuts, make-ahead or freezing hints, serving tips, and healthful suggestions. We hope we have updated the simple, homey fare of our childhood in such a way as to create something more stylishly appealing for today's palates and life styles, yet true to a tradition of old-fashioned, "real food" comfort. We like to think that Mother and Grandma would be pleased.

Using this Book

In writing the recipes for this book, we have made every attempt to explain clearly how to prepare and cook the dish. We realize, however, that there are a great number of variables involved in any culinary process that cannot be entirely accounted for or controlled.

Cooking equipment can vary dramatically. Ovens employ a variety of heating technologies that produce differing results; stovetop burners can vary considerably in their manner and intensity of heating. The different materials from which cookware is made all have varying degrees of heat conductivity that can affect cooking times. And, not even all measuring spoons or cups are calibrated equally.

Similar disparities can be found in the ingredients themselves: For example, flours often vary one from another, the same cuts of meat can vary in tenderness, different brands of yogurt vary in sharpness, eggs may vary in size even within the same carton, and herbs will vary pungency depending on age or other factors. We could go on, but you get the idea. And then there is the matter of taste: One person's salty, sweet, or spicy is another person's bland.

As an aid, we have incorporated time and temperature suggestions and often multiple measures as well, e.g. cups plus weight. The recipes in this book represent the way we have made these dishes. We credit our readers, however, with a general culinary savvy and common sense and trust that you will approach the recipes not as rigid requirements but guidelines and thus feel free to adapt them to your own kitchen circumstances, equipment, and ingredient preferences.

To the specific instructions given in the recipes we would like to add a few further notes of a general nature regarding ingredients and procedures:

- When we call for butter we assume unsalted butter
- When we call for eggs we assume large size
- When we call for salt we assume supermarket brand iodized salt
- Unless otherwise indicated, milk is considered to be whole milk
- Vegetables are assumed to be fresh rather than canned or frozen
- Unless otherwise specified, flour is all-purpose
- Pepper is freshly ground; nutmeg and Parmesan are freshly grated
- Three to one is a good rule of thumb ratio for fresh herbs to dried
- Our favorite herb, cilantro, is also known as coriander
- Hazelnuts are also known as filberts
- When no size is specified, assume medium
- For broadest application, our testing was done using good quality, generally available cookware and home-standard ovens and burners

APPETIZERS &
HORS D'OEUVRES

When we look at the food that we cook and trace its origins back to what Grandma made, the area in which we have departed from our culinary heritage most dramatically is appetizers or hors d'oeuvres. It wasn't that Grandma didn't like or didn't eat small nibbly things. It was just that she didn't drink—except for a bedtime nip of Sherry or fruit-flavored liqueur—and thus a cocktail hour with hors-d'oeuvre offerings was not part of her concept of dining. (We suspect that Grandpa's tendency to overindulge and the desire to remove temptation were motivating factors as well, but, as children, it took us years to figure this out.) Although we share Grandma's general preference for entertaining friends with dinner rather than a cocktail party, we do offer guests pre-dinner drinks along with a few appetizers. On our own, however, we also love the idea of eating bits of this and that and will often make a family meal of a few little plates of things we would normally serve as hors d'oeuvres—and that Grandma might have thought of as teatime snacks.

TEX-MEX CHEX

2 tablespoons garlic powder

1 tablespoon dried oregano

2 teaspoons chili powder

1 teaspoon ground cumin

1 teaspoon dried thyme

1 teaspoon crumbled dried rosemary

2 teaspoons salt

6 tablespoons butter

2 tablespoons Worcestershire sauce

6 cups mixed Chex-type cereal

3 cups small cheese crackers (fish shapes are especially nice)

2 cups small pretzels such as thin sticks or tiny twists

1 cup peanuts (or mixed nuts if you are feeling extravagant)

From the very first time we tried the Ralston Purina company's Chex Party Mix, that addictive snack made its appearance at every family gathering. The recipe Mother took from the Chex cereal box, which she followed to a T, called for only Chex, nuts, butter, Worcestershire sauce, and seasoned salt. We prefer more zip, however, often adding other ingredients plus prodigious quantities of chili powder, cumin, and garlic. Having prepared bushels of our spicier concoctions over the years, we continue the family tradition with Tex-Mex Chex and Chinese Chex. The southwestern version holds its own nicely against a frosty ale as a Super Bowl party warm-up, and our favorite Asian-style combo is a great snack while waiting for the Chinese takeout order to arrive.

Preheat the oven to 250° F. In a small bowl stir together the garlic powder, oregano, chili powder, cumin, thyme, rosemary, and salt. In a large metal baking pan (about 10 by 13 inches) melt the butter, add the Worcestershire sauce, and combine the mixture well. Add the Chex cereal, crackers, pretzels, and nuts to the pan and combine the mixture carefully until the Chex mixture is well coated with the butter mixture. Sprinkle half the spice mixture over the Chex mixture, stir it in gently, then sprinkle and stir in the remaining spice mixture until all the Chex mixture is evenly coated with the butter mixture and spices. Bake the Chex mix, stirring gently every 10 minutes, for 45 minutes, or until it is well crisped. Let the Chex mix cool completely in the pan and store it in an airtight container. Makes about 12 cups.

P&B's Hints: We've been told the Chex Mix keeps well when stored in an airtight container and freezes well too, but we've never had a batch last long enough to find out.

CHINESE CHEX

Preheat the oven to 250° F. In a small bowl stir together the chili powder, garlic powder, ginger, basil, five-spice powder, and salt. In a large metal baking pan (about 10 by 13 inches) melt the butter, add the soy sauce and sesame oil, and combine the mixture well. Add the Chex cereal, chow mein noodles (broken if very long), sesame sticks, and cashews and combine the mixture carefully until the Chex mixture is well coated with the butter mixture. Sprinkle half the spice mixture over the Chex mixture, stir the two together gently, then sprinkle and stir in the remaining spice mixture until all the Chex mixture is evenly coated with the butter mixture and spices. Bake the Chex mix, stirring gently every 10 minutes, for 45 minutes, or until it is well crisped. Let the Chex mix cool completely in the pan and store it in an airtight container. Makes about 12 cups.

4 teaspoons chili powder

4 teaspoons garlic powder

4 teaspoons powdered ginger

4 teaspoons crumbled dried basil

1 teaspoon Chinese five-spice powder

1 teaspoon salt

6 tablespoons butter

2 tablespoons soy sauce

1 tablespoon Asian sesame oil

6 cups rice/corn Chex-type cereal

3 cups ¼-inch-thick chow mein noodles (6-ounce package)

2 cups sesame sticks (7-ounce package)

1 cup cashew halves

SOUTHWEST CHEESE WAFERS

1½ cups (about 6 ounces) grated very sharp aged Cheddar (do not use packaged shredded cheese)

1 stick (½ cup) butter, softened

1 cup all-purpose flour

½ teaspoon ground cumin

¼ teaspoon chipotle chile powder

½ teaspoon salt

¾ cup finely crushed corn Chex or corn flakes cereal

½ cup finely ground pistachios or almonds

Grandma, Mother, and just about any other home cook we've ever known has some sort of crispy cheese wafer in her repertoire. This hors d'oeuvre, long a staple of community cookbooks, still graces cocktail tables with predictable regularity. Here is the latest version of our ever-evolving family recipe.

In the bowl of a food processor blend the cheese and butter until they are just combined. Add the flour (sifted together with the cumin, chile powder, and salt) and process the mixture, pulsing and scraping down the sides of the bowl as necessary, until it is combined and starts to form a ball. Add the crushed cereal and nuts and process the mixture until it is well combined and forms a cohesive ball. Preheat the oven to 350° F. Shape the dough into 1-inch balls, set them 2 inches apart on nonstick baking sheets, and with a fork flatten them gently in a crosshatch pattern. Bake the wafers, in batches if necessary, for 15 minutes, or until they are lightly browned and crisp. Let the wafers cool completely on a rack and store them in an airtight container. Makes about 60 wafers.

P&B's Hints: The prepared dough, either in one piece or shaped into balls, can be made ahead and kept, wrapped in plastic wrap, in the refrigerator for several days.

HORS-D'OEUVRE TOAST CUPS

Many of the hors d'oeuvres or appetizers we now serve originated from things that Grandma made for teatime. Among these were toasts topped with various spreads such as egg, chicken, tuna, or shrimp salad. Although we generally use store-bought crackers or toasts as a base for spreadable toppings, these mini toast cups are more versatile and make a more elegant presentation. They take a little time and effort to create but are worth the trouble for a fancier occasion as they can be made ahead and extras store well, ready for last-minute entertaining.

Preheat the oven to 350° F. Trim off and discard any very dark bread crusts and from each slice of bread cut out 2 rounds. The remaining scraps can be used for making buttered bread crumbs (page 111)—it's what Grandma would have done. Spray one side of the rounds very lightly with cooking spray and fit a round, sprayed side down, into each cup of the mini muffin tin, pressing the round firmly into the bottom edges of the muffin cup and gently against the sides. Bake the bread cups in the oven, in as many batches as necessary, for 10 minutes, or until they are lightly browned and crisp. Let the cups cool completely on a rack and store them in an airtight container. One loaf makes about 60 hors-d'oeuvre toast cups.

1 loaf of extra-thin-sliced white bread (we prefer Pepperidge Farm)

flavorless cooking spray

EQUIPMENT:
mini muffin tins

a 1¾- to 2-inch round cookie cutter (or use a can with top and bottom removed)

P&B's Hints: Some of our favorite hors-d'oeuvre fillings for the toast cups include guacamole, sour cream and caviar, hummus, cream cheese and smoked salmon, tapenade, and caponata. The toast cups can also be made in a larger size and filled with a variety of things such as scrambled egg combinations for brunch, creamed chicken for lunch, or seafood Newburg for a first course.

SPICED WALNUTS

1 pound walnut halves

½ cup sugar

2½ tablespoons canola oil

1½ teaspoons ground cumin

½ teaspoon salt

⅓ teaspoon curry powder

¼ teaspoon chipotle chile powder

¼ teaspoon powdered ginger

¼ teaspoon ground coriander

¼ teaspoon ground cloves

Grandma was extremely fond of walnuts, and they figured prominently in a number of her cakes and cookies. We can remember long hours in her kitchen, helping to crack open walnut shells with an old-fashioned squeeze-handle nutcracker and removing the nutmeats with a sharp metal pick. Happily that nutcracker was long ago retired, and we now make this hors d'oeuvre with packaged shelled walnuts. Whereas Grandma tended to make cinnamon-sugared or pickled walnuts, we love the crisp texture of these baked nuts and the way their slight sweetness is set off by a heady blend of spices.

Preheat the oven to 325° F. In a saucepan of boiling water boil the walnuts for 1 minute and drain them well in a colander. In a bowl toss the nuts while they are still hot with the sugar and the oil until they are well coated. Arrange the nuts in one layer in a nonstick baking pan (about 17 by 11 inches), bake them, stirring well every 5 minutes, for 20 minutes, or until they are browned and crisp, and transfer them to a bowl large enough for easy tossing. In a small bowl combine well the cumin, salt, curry powder, chile powder, ginger, coriander, and clove. Sprinkle the spices, half at a time, over the warm nuts, tossing the mixture together until the nuts are evenly coated with the spices. Spread the nuts in one layer on a sheet of foil, let them cool completely, and store them in an airtight container. Makes about 4 cups.

WHITE BEAN SPREAD

The closest Grandma came to serving pre-dinner nibbles was a cut-glass dish of simple crudités: celery and carrot sticks with perhaps some pitted black olives. These usually made their appearance on the dining table and were almost more a part of the table setting than an appetizer. If the meal was running late due to the roast taking longer to cook than anticipated, for example, the unadorned vegetable sticks kept us going until the main course arrived. We often serve our guests crudités—a bit more elaborate than Grandma's however—with pre-dinner drinks. Though Grandma might not favor the cocktailing, we feel sure she would have enjoyed dipping her simple crudités into this southwest-accented spread.

In a small skillet cook the onion and garlic in the oil over moderately low heat, stirring occasionally, until they are softened. Add the cumin and chile powder and cook the mixture, stirring occasionally, until the onion is very soft. In a food processor purée the beans with the onion mixture until the two are well combined. Add the lemon juice, rind, and salt and purée the mixture until it is smooth. Gently blend in the cilantro and transfer the mixture to a serving dish. Serve the spread with vegetable crudités for dipping or as a topping for pita wedges or crackers. Makes about 2 cups.

1 small onion, minced

1 garlic clove, minced

2 teaspoons olive oil

1 teaspoon ground cumin

¼ teaspoon chipotle chile powder (optional)

two 15- to 16-ounce cans of Great Northern (white) beans, drained and rinsed

1 tablespoon lemon juice

¼ teaspoon grated lemon rind

¾ teaspoon salt, or to taste

1 tablespoon minced cilantro

crudités, pita wedges, or crackers as an accompaniment

> **P&B's Hints:** Adjust the amount of spicing and flavoring to your taste. Try adding well-drained, minced sun-dried tomato packed in oil or snipped fresh chives. Substitute parsley for the cilantro or sprinkle minced herbs on top for a fancier look. Put the mixture into pita pockets with chopped tomato, red onion, and shredded lettuce for a light vegetarian lunch.

SMOKED SALMON MOUSSE WITH DILL

1 packet unflavored gelatin (about 2 teaspoons)

¾ cup sour cream

3 tablespoons mayonnaise

¼ cup minced scallion

3 hard-boiled eggs, coarsely chopped

3 teaspoons lemon juice

¼ teaspoon grated lemon rind

1 teaspoon Dijon-style mustard

6 ounces (¾ cup) minced smoked salmon

1 tablespoon minced dill plus sprigs for garnish

a couple drops hot pepper sauce

Both Grandma and Mother made salmon loaf, concocted with canned salmon, crushed Saltine crackers, milk, and eggs—all everyday household staples. We ate it both hot and cold. Although tasty enough, it wasn't a dish to get excited about. Dining out over the years, we enjoyed a variety of lighter, fluffier, and more elegant salmon soufflés and mousses. These dishes, however, all seemed far too labor-intensive or time-critical to undertake making at home. Through much experimentation, we came up with this simple make-ahead hors-d'oeuvre mousse—more interesting than Grandma's loaf but far less trouble than those restaurant preparations.

In a small microwave dish sprinkle the gelatin over 2 tablespoons water and let it soften for 3 minutes. Heat the mixture in a microwave for a total of 30 seconds, stopping and stirring once halfway through, and stir the mixture until the gelatin is completely dissolved. In a food processor blend together the sour cream, mayonnaise, scallion, egg, lemon juice, rind, and mustard until the mixture is smooth and transfer it to a bowl. Stir in the gelatin, salmon, dill, and hot pepper sauce. Line a 2-cup mold with plastic wrap, pressing it smoothly against the sides and leaving enough overhang to cover the top, pour the salmon mixture into the mold, carefully cover it with the overhang, and chill it for at least 3 hours, or until it is completely set. The mousse can be made a day or two in advance and kept covered and chilled. Uncover the mousse, invert a serving plate over it, and invert the mousse onto the serving plate. Peel off the plastic wrap carefully and serve the mousse, garnished with a sprig of dill if desired, with a small spreader and crackers or small toasts. Serves 8 to 10.

P&B's Hints: The mousse works just fine, too, made with fat-free or low-fat sour cream and mayo. If you are entertaining on back-to-back occasions, divide the mousse between two 1-cup molds for easy two-for-one party planning. The mousse can also be made in mini-muffin tins (sprayed with flavorless cooking spray) and served unmolded onto a bed of lettuce as an elegant appetizer course.

CRAB MEAT SKINNY DIP

Mother and daddy didn't share Grandma's temperance stance and would occasionally host a cocktail party, serving Manhattans, which were all the rage at the time. (We got our introduction to hard liquor in the form of the alcohol-soaked maraschino cherries that garnished these concoctions.) The accompanying hors d'oeuvres usually included a tray of cheese and crackers, maybe a cheese ball if it was holiday time, and the ever-popular dip made with sour cream and onion soup mix. After working our way through gallons of that dip and various packaged cheese spreads in our post-college years, we ultimately moved on to healthier and more sophisticated fare. Though we call this creation skinny dip, it is really more of a spread and it can be made less "skinny" and more unctuous by using low- or full-fat products. It is light and elegant, and, because lump crab meat is something of an extravagance these days, we reserve it for special occasions and guests we really like.

¼ cup fat-free cream cheese, softened

¼ cup fat-free or low-fat mayonnaise

¼ cup fat-free sour cream

1 teaspoon packed grated lime rind

2 teaspoons fresh lime juice

2 tablespoons minced cilantro

1 pound lump crab meat, drained of any juices and picked over

In a bowl cream together the cream cheese, mayonnaise, and sour cream and stir in the rind, lime juice, and cilantro. Add the crab meat and fold the mixture together gently so as not to mash up the crab meat until the mixture is well combined. Serve the spread with crackers or small toasts. Makes about 2½ cups.

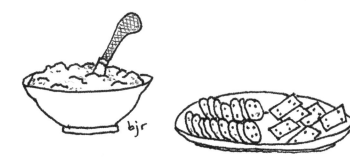

> **P&B's Hints:** Scoops of this "spread" nestled in a bed of lettuce and accompanied by Kirby cucumber rounds, grape tomatoes, and avocado slices make a lovely first course or summer luncheon salad. The spread is also a great filling for tea sandwiches.

SPICY MEAT EMPANADAS

½ pound ground beef or pork or a combination

¾ cup minced onion

1 tablespoon vegetable oil

¼ cup minced red bell pepper

2 large garlic cloves, minced

1 teaspoon sweet paprika (preferably smoked Spanish paprika)

1 teaspoon ground cumin

¾ teaspoon cinnamon

½ teaspoon salt

3 tablespoons ketchup

¼ cup raisins or currants

¼ cup minced olives (green, black, or oil-cured)

1 hard-boiled egg, finely chopped

2 tablespoons minced cilantro

masa harina or flour for rolling out dough

2 refrigerated ready-made 9-inch pie crusts

1 egg, beaten well

Grandma always seemed to have lumps of leftover dough, trimmings cut from pie crusts and pastries. So that they didn't go to waste (the W word was a cardinal sin in our family), she would re-roll the dough and use even odd-shaped pieces of it to enclose bits of either sweet or savory filling. Everything from chopped nuts with cinnamon sugar to extra meatloaf mix were encased in dough and baked into tasty treats. We thought Grandma had invented these little turnovers until we encountered similar creations throughout Latin and South America, generally known as empanadas. We don't have a lot of leftover pastry dough lying about in our kitchens these days, but our love of these snacks often spurs us on to make frequent batches of spicy empanadas with refrigerated store-bought pie crust or a simple masa harina dough made according to the package directions. Empanadas can be made in various sizes to suit your needs; and, unbaked, they freeze well to have on hand for hors d'oeuvres, a quick snack, or light lunch.

In a skillet cook the meat over moderately high heat, breaking up the lumps, until it is no longer pink and transfer it to a bowl, draining off any fat. In the skillet cook the onion in the oil over moderate heat, stirring occasionally, until it is softened slightly, add the bell pepper, garlic, paprika, and cumin, and cook the mixture, stirring occasionally, until the vegetables are softened. Stir in the cinnamon, salt, ketchup, raisins, olives, egg, and cilantro and combine the mixture with the meat. Sprinkle a working surface with masa harina, lay one of the pie crusts on the surface, and sprinkle it with more masa harina. Roll out the dough about 1/16 inch thick and cut it into 3½-inch rounds. Gather the scraps, re-roll them, and cut out more rounds. Each pie crust should make 12 to 15 rounds. Preheat the oven to 375° F. Spoon a tablespoon of filling in the center of each round, moisten the edges of the dough with water, and fold the dough over the filling to make a half moon shape, pressing the edges together on both sides with the tines of a fork. Brush the empanadas with the beaten egg, arrange them on baking sheets, and bake them for 25 minutes, or until they are lightly browned and cooked through. Prepare and bake more empanadas with the remaining pie crust in the same manner. Serve the empanadas hot, warm, or at room temperature. Makes about 2 dozen 3½-inch empanadas.

ANTIPASTO BITES

Though Grandma generally frowned on drinking alcohol before, during, or after dinner, Mother and Daddy enjoyed their evening Manhattans, along with a simple hors d'oeuvre or two. More wine drinkers than cocktailers, we like to start off an Italianate meal with an antipasto-style appetizer as we sip our glass of Soave or Sangiovese. Inspired by the sumptuous array of meats, cheeses, and vegetables laid out in a tempting display at many Italian restaurants, we ultimately came up with this homemade version: a blend of various common antipasto selections in bite-size form.

In a microwaveable bowl combine all the ingredients and microwave the mixture, stirring twice, for 2 minutes, or until the mozzarella is melted enough to bind the mixture together lightly. Let the mixture come to room temperature and spoon heaping teaspoons of it into hors d'oeuvre toast cups (page 15) or packaged mini filo cups (available in the frozen foods case of large supermarkets). Makes about 24 hors d'oeuvres.

½ cup finely minced cured Italian meat such as salami, pepperoni, hot sopressata, or prosciutto

¼ cup finely shredded mozzarella

2 tablespoons minced or coarsely grated Parmesan cheese

2 tablespoons minced green bell pepper

1 tablespoon minced celery

1 tablespoon seeded and minced Roma tomato

1 tablespoon minced scallion or chives

1 tablespoon minced black olive

1 to 2 teaspoons seeded and minced pepperoncini (optional)

1 tablespoon minced fresh basil or basil pesto or 1 teaspoon dried basil

1 teaspoon extra virgin olive oil

½ teaspoon dried oregano

P&B's Hints: The filling mixture can be made up to one day ahead and kept covered and chilled. For best flavor let the chilled mixture come to room temperature before serving.

SALSA BRUSCHETTA

1 French bread baguette, sliced on a slight diagonal ¼-inch thick

mild olive oil

garlic salt

1 pound plum tomatoes, seeded and finely diced (about 2¼ cups)

1 yellow bell pepper, finely diced (about ⅔ cup)

⅓ cup minced scallion

⅓ cup minced cilantro

1 large garlic clove, minced and mashed to a paste with ½ teaspoon salt

2 tablespoons fresh lime juice

1 tablespoon extra virgin olive oil

1 avocado (preferably Haas)

Ever thrifty, Grandma was especially resourceful in putting stale bread to good use. Full slices were transformed into French toast, cubed pieces went into bread pudding, thin oven-crisped triangles or rounds became the base of teatime canapés, and any remaining scraps were turned into crumbs for topping baked dishes. An inherited thrift gene apparently lives on in us, as we carefully slice up and toast leftover French bread for our own canapés. We have, however, expanded on Grandma's limited canapé repertoire with a multinational mix of flavors. At the height of tomato season this luscious hors d'oeuvre appears frequently in our houses.

Preheat the oven to 350° F. Brush one side of the bread slices lightly with mild olive oil, sprinkle the oiled surface with garlic salt, and arrange the slices on a baking sheet. Toast the slices, in batches if necessary, turning them once, until they are crisp and very lightly browned then let them cool on a rack. In a nonreactive bowl combine the tomatoes, yellow pepper, scallion, and cilantro. In a small bowl stir together the garlic paste, lime juice, and extra virgin olive oil, add the mixture to the tomato mixture, and toss the salsa together lightly until it is well combined. (The salsa can be made up to this point a day ahead and kept, covered and chilled, though it is really better served fresh.) Just before serving, add the avocado, peeled and finely diced. Top each of the toasts, garlic side up, with a heaping spoonful of the salsa. Serves 6 to 8.

P&B's Hints: Most baguettes will make more toasts than you need for this recipe—the extras keep well, stored in an airtight container. We love the garlic-bread taste of the toasts, but if you prefer, the bread can be toasted plain and then will be more versatile. We also often add ½ cup finely diced mozzarella to the tomato mixture.

ASIAN-ACCENTED EGGPLANT SPREAD

Eggplant is rarely in contention for top honors as anyone's favorite vegetable, and so it was in our house. That said, over the years we have developed a fondness for eggplant, also known abroad as aubergine, where it enjoys greater popularity. Grandma incorporated the vegetable into any number of ratatouille-style combinations, and Mother occasionally served it well obscured under layers of Parmesan and marinara sauce in a nod to Italy. Now that most major supermarkets carry a selection of seasonings from the Far East, we often like to give some of our eggplant dishes an Asian flavor, as in this easy, make-ahead hors-d'oeuvre spread.

Prick the eggplant in several places with the tines of a fork and in a microwave cook it, set on a rack over several layers of paper towels, on high power for 7 minutes. Turn the eggplant over and cook it for 7 minutes more, or until it is soft and deflated. When the eggplant is cool enough to handle, halve it lengthwise, scoop out the flesh, and discard the skin and stem. Blot up the excess moisture from the flesh with paper towels and transfer the eggplant to a food processor. In a small saucepan heat the garlic, scallion, and ginger in the sesame oil over moderately low heat, stirring, for several minutes, or until the garlic is softened slightly. Add the soy sauce and mirin and heat the mixture, stirring, until it is warmed and fragrant. In the food processor blend the eggplant, the garlic mixture, and the cilantro until the mixture is well combined but still slightly chunky. Spoon the mixture into a serving bowl and chill it, covered, for up to 3 days. Serve the spread cold or at room temperature with crackers (rice crackers are nice) or small toasts. Makes about 2 cups.

1 medium eggplant, about 1¼ pounds

1 large garlic clove, crushed and minced

⅓ cup minced white part scallion or mild onion

1 tablespoon peeled and minced gingerroot

2¼ teaspoons Asian sesame oil

1 tablespoon soy sauce

1 tablespoon mirin (Japanese sweetened rice wine), sake, or mild rice vinegar

¼ cup minced cilantro, or to taste

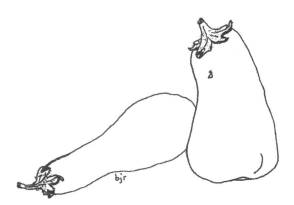

SAUSACHOKE SPIRALS

½ pound sausage meat (your favorite bulk Italian or spicy breakfast blend)

a 6½-ounce jar marinated artichoke hearts, drained well

an 8-ounce tube refrigerated crescent rolls

Grandma whipped up batches of her wonderfully flaky pastry dough on almost a daily basis, using it for everything from humble pot pies to elegant desserts, as well as a host of savory snacks. When it comes to savory snacks or finger food, more often than not we rely on frozen pie crust or puff pastry or those super-versatile refrigerated crescent rolls. Ever on the lookout for uncomplicated, make-ahead hors d'oeuvres, we have stuffed the crescent roll dough with every imaginable (and unimaginable) filling. We always like to keep a sausachoke roll in the freezer so we can quickly bake up spirals for drop-in guests.

In a small skillet sauté the sausage meat over moderate heat, stirring and breaking it up, until it is lightly browned. Transfer the sausage with a slotted spoon to paper towels to drain and discard the fat in the skillet. Cut off and discard any tough leaves from the artichoke hearts and chop the hearts coarsely. In a food processor pulse together the sausage and artichokes until the mixture is well combined but still slightly chunky. (The filling can be made up to several days in advance and stored, covered and chilled.) Preheat the oven to 375° F. Separate the crescent dough into 4 squares and press the dough together to seal the diagonal perforations. Spread each square with a thin layer of the filling (2 to 3 tablespoons), leaving a ½-inch border at one end and pressing the filling lightly into the dough with back of a spoon. Brush the border with a little water and, starting at the non-border end, roll up the squares firmly but not too tightly, pressing the seam against the roll to seal the rolls closed. (The rolls can be frozen, well wrapped, at this point for later use.) Slice each roll crosswise into ¼-inch rounds, arrange the spirals about 1½ inches apart on ungreased baking sheets, and bake them for 12 to 14 minutes, or until they are nicely browned. Transfer the spirals with a spatula to racks to crisp for a minute or two then serve them warm or at room temperature. (The baked spirals can be cooled and stored, well wrapped in plastic and chilled, for up to 2 days and reheated in a preheated 325° F. oven for 5 to 7 minutes.) Makes about 60 hors d'oeuvres.

P&B's Hints: Any leftover filling is delicious cooked into scrambled eggs or mixed with an equal amount of cream cheese and spread on crackers.

PARTY PINWHEELS

Some of the culinary creations we have come up with over the years are not updates or variations of a particular dish that Grandma made. Rather, they have grown out of some remembered component of a dish or technique she used, which we have applied in an entirely different context. These tasty morsels, for example, owe their inspiration to Grandma's irresistible date pinwheel cookies and various roll-up nut pastries. In our hands the pinwheel idea leap-frogged into appetizer mode and married with today's sandwich wrap craze, resulting in these make-ahead hors d'oeuvres. We use packaged wraps for these elegant-looking yet super-easy pinwheels, and the filling is limited only by your taste preferences and imagination. Here are some of our favorite combinations.

THE BASICS:
4 ounces cream cheese (fat-free, low-fat, or full-fat), softened

a 10-inch wrap (any flavor of your choosing)

Spread the cream cheese evenly over the entire surface of the wrap, sprinkle the desired filling mixture evenly over it to within ¼ inch of the edges, and roll the wrap up tightly around the filling into a log, pressing the edges gently onto the log to help it stay closed. Chill the log, tightly enclosed in plastic wrap, for at least an hour or overnight. Remove the plastic wrap, trim off the ragged ends of the log (eat the trimmings), and slice the log crosswise into ½-inch pinwheels. Makes 16 to 18 hors d'oeuvres.

CAVIAR PINWHEELS: Sprinkle the cream cheese with 2 teaspoons minced chives, a 2-ounce jar of red lumpfish or salmon caviar, and 1 finely crumbled hard-boiled egg yolk.

SALMON DILL PINWHEELS: Sprinkle the cream cheese with 1 teaspoon minced chives, 1 tablespoon minced dill, and about ⅓ cup minced smoked salmon.

CURRIED CHICKEN PINWHEELS: Mix ½ teaspoon curry powder and 1 tablespoon finely minced chutney into the cream cheese before spreading it on the wrap and sprinkle cream cheese with 1 tablespoon minced cilantro and ⅓ cup finely minced cooked chicken.

PEPPERONI OLIVE PINWHEELS: Sprinkle the cream cheese with 2 teaspoons minced flat-leafed parsley and ⅓ cup each finely ground pepperoni and minced oil-cured black olives.

NUTTY BLUE CHEESE PINWHEELS: Sprinkle the cream cheese with ⅓ cup finely crumbled blue cheese, 2 tablespoons currants, and 2 tablespoons finely chopped toasted walnuts.

SPINACH AND FETA SQUARES

1 cup finely chopped onion

1 large garlic clove, minced

1 tablespoon butter

3 eggs

1 cup milk

1 cup flour

2 teaspoons baking powder

1 tablespoon minced fresh thyme or 1 teaspoon dried

4 tablespoons minced fresh basil or 1 tablespoon crumbled dried

½ teaspoon freshly grated nutmeg

a 10-ounce package frozen chopped spinach, thawed and squeezed dry

1 cup crumbled Feta cheese (about 6 ounces)

1 cup grated Monterey Jack cheese with jalapeño (about 4 ounces)

Mother's original recipe, which she would make when the onions or scallions in the garden needed thinning and the spinach was threatening to take over the whole backyard, used a container of cottage cheese. When Feta became a common grocery store commodity, we all agreed that its tangy saltiness was a huge improvement over that boring old cottage cheese or Grandma's standby farmers cheese. A little Monterey Jack with jalapeño then added further excitement for jaded adult palates.

Preheat the oven to 350° F. In a small saucepan cook the onion and garlic in the butter over moderately low heat, stirring occasionally, until they are softened. In a large bowl beat the eggs with the milk until the mixture is well blended, stir in the flour, baking powder, thyme, basil, and nutmeg, then fold in the onion mixture, spinach, and cheeses. Spread the mixture in a 9- by 12-inch baking dish, well coated with cooking spray, and bake it for 30 minutes, or until the top is lightly browned and the mixture pulls away slightly from the sides of the dish. Let the mixture cool in the dish on a rack for a few minutes and cut it into bite-size squares for hors d'oeuvres or larger squares for brunch. Serve the squares hot, at room temperature, or chilled. Serves 12 as an hors d'oeuvre or 6 as a brunch dish.

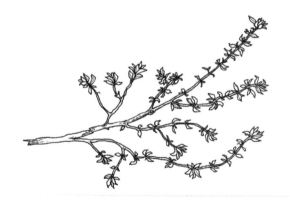

P&B's Hints: Fold 1 cup of cooked, crumbled sausage into the spinach mixture for a hearty one-dish meal. The dish freezes well and reheats nicely in the microwave.

GRINGO POPCORN

As far back as we can remember we have always loved popcorn. It was a food that was both fun to cook (watching the kernels magically pop) and fun to consume (eating with our hands instead of silverware). Daddy was in charge of popcorn, as it was usually a fireside treat and roughly qualified as campfire cooking. The dried corn kernels were placed in a long-handled rectangular wire basket, which had a pull-back sliding lid, and the basket was held and shaken over fireplace coals until the kernels had all popped. The slightly smoky popcorn was then tossed in a bowl with lots of melted butter and salt. Our cooking methods may differ these days, but the siren call of popcorn still seduces us. Today we lighten things up with "better fat" canola oil and liven up the taste with an array of spicy/smoky seasonings.

¼ cup canola oil

1 teaspoon mild smoked paprika

1½ teaspoons ground cumin

½ teaspoon chipotle chile powder

½ teaspoon garlic salt, or to taste

½ cup popcorn kernels

In a kettle stir together the oil, paprika, cumin, chile powder, and garlic salt and stir in the popcorn kernels, coating them well. Cook the mixture over high heat, stirring and shaking the kettle, until the kernels begin to pop. Cover the kettle with the lid and continue to cook the mixture, swirling and shaking the kettle often to coat the kernels evenly with the oil mixture, until the popping has stopped. Remove the kettle from the heat, transfer the popcorn mixture to a bowl, and toss it, adding extra salt if desired, until it is well combined with the seasoning evenly distributed. Serves 4 to 6.

P&B's Hints: Make a triple batch of the paprika/cumin/chile powder/garlic salt mixture and keep it in a shaker jar. When tight for time, we have been known to sprinkle the mixture on freshly made microwave popcorn. The mixture is also great for seasoning chicken cutlets or pork chops.

SOUP

We had homemade soups virtually every week when we were growing up, and most had their origin in Sunday's midday dinner, which had a traditional format and comforting consistency. After a quick breakfast, we would set the dining table with the good china and Mother would pop something into the oven to roast while we were at church. (A similar scenario would take place at Grandma's if we were headed there for the big meal of the week.) Upon our return from church, we'd be greeted by incredible aromas filling the house and a meal that was on the table within minutes. Turkey, chicken, pot roast, and ham—especially ham—comprised the usual roster of Sunday staples. Then on Monday and Tuesday came turkey tetrazzini, chicken salad, beef hash, or ham croquettes. And, by midweek, the stock pot was simmering. Big bowls of homemade soup, served with either Mother's freshly baked bread or Grandma's buttermilk biscuits, are among our fondest gastronomic memories. In Mother's last year, when few meals offered even the slightest temptation, variations on her homemade soups were always welcomed and consumed with a smile.

bjr

CHICKEN STOCK

the carcass of a roast chicken

2 carrots, trimmed and cut into chunks

2 large celery stalks, cut into pieces

1 large onion, root end cut away and the unpeeled onion quartered (the skin gives a richer color to the stock) and stuck with a clove if desired

1 large unpeeled garlic clove, crushed slightly

1 bay leaf

1 leek, halved lengthwise, washed well, and cut into 2-inch lengths

6 peppercorns (optional)

a handful of parsley sprigs

a cheesecloth bundle or sachet packet of dried herbs (optional)

Don't flip the page and pass this recipe by! Give it a try, and we think you'll be glad you did. Chicken stock is not something that most of us realistically consider making from scratch on a regular basis. When it is called for in a dish, we admit that we generally auto-pilot to the pantry shelf and reach for our supply of good quality canned broth. Mother and Grandma did not always have this option, and they made chicken stock (as well as meat, fish, and vegetable stocks) virtually every week. It is undeniably the main reason that their soups and stews were so memorable. Once you've made a soup or stew with homemade stock, you can easily get spoiled. So, some rainy Saturday or evening when you will be around the house for a couple hours, pull out this recipe. Chicken stock is not rocket science and precise measurements or the choice of what goes into it is REALLY flexible. In addition to the basic ingredients listed here, we often will "clean out the refrigerator," tossing in leftover vegetables, ham, or kielbasa, and adding any juices from canned or cooked vegetables as well. We are fortunate enough to have more freezer space than the minuscule ice-cube storage compartment of Grandma's refrigerator and thus have the luxury of knowing that a supply of homemade stock is ready and waiting whenever the craving hits for a really great old-fashioned bowl of soup.

In a stockpot or large kettle combine all of the ingredients with 14 cups water and bring the water to a boil over high heat. Reduce the heat to moderately low and cook the stock at a bubbling simmer, occasionally stirring and skimming any fat and froth that rises to the surface, for at least 2 hours. Let the stock cool in the kettle for 30 minutes then strain it through a fine-holed colander or heavy strainer into a large bowl and discard the solids. Chill the stock, covered, for several hours or overnight and remove any fat from the surface. The stock keeps, covered, in the refrigerator for several days and freezes well. Makes about 8 cups.

P&B's Hints: By the way, you don't need to roast a chicken for this recipe; the carcass of a rotisserie bird bought from the deli counter is generally what generally goes into our stock.

EGG DROP SOUP

Grandma and Mother's chicken noodle soup was the peerless cure-all of our childhood, whether restoring an ailing body or downcast spirit. Through our world travels in later years—as well as trips to various neighborhood Chinese restaurants—we learned that other cultures had their own versions of this broth-based curative. Chinese congee (rice gruel, which tastes better than it sounds) and egg drop soup fall into this category. Quick and easy to make, egg drop soup is a dish we now often turn to for a light pick-me-up, be it physical or psychological.

3 cups chicken stock or broth

1 teaspoon Asian sesame oil

1 tablespoon cornstarch, dissolved in 2 tablespoons broth or water

1 egg, beaten

2 tablespoons very thinly sliced scallion, or to taste

In a saucepan bring the stock and sesame oil to a boil over moderately high heat, stir the cornstarch mixture to recombine it, and stir it into the stock mixture. Cook the mixture, stirring, until it is thickened slightly. Remove the pan from the heat and add the beaten egg in a slow stream, stirring so that you get thin shreds of cooked egg. Add the scallion and salt to taste if necessary. Serves 2 or 3.

P&B's Hints: The secret to perfect texture in this soup is to make sure that you don't overcook the egg. We often augment this basic egg-and-broth mixture with finely diced cooked chicken or shrimp, a variety of chopped cooked vegetables or canned creamed corn, any of those mini soup pastas that cook almost instantly, and a sprinkling of cilantro.

SPLIT PEA SOUP

4 to 5 cups ham stock, chicken stock, or chicken broth

1¼ cups green split peas, rinsed and picked over

1 cup diced kielbasa

¾ cup diced celery

¾ cup diced carrot

½ cup diced onion

1 large garlic clove, minced

1 teaspoon crumbled dried basil

1 teaspoon dried tarragon

1 teaspoon dried thyme

1 bay leaf

4 whole cloves

½ teaspoon salt

4 drops hot pepper sauce (optional)

4 drops liquid smoke (optional but nice, especially if you've used chicken stock or broth)

Of all the soups that originated with Sunday dinner's leftover ham bone, split pea was our wintertime favorite. Perhaps its sweet, warm greenness was a reminder of spring—or maybe it's just that the soup is so soothingly good. Since Grandma had neither a blender nor food processor, she used her potato masher to achieve a naturally chunky texture. If you like a smoother version, just purée a portion of the cooked soup and then add it back to the pot. We both like the soup to have recognizable bits of meat and vegetable, but Bonnie tends to be more of a masher and Pat more of a purée-er. As we rarely have a leftover ham bone (or supply of ham stock) on hand these days, we generally use chicken broth and flavor the soup with kielbasa sausage and a bit more herbs and spicing than Grandma or Mother used. Served with garlic toast, corn bread, or breadsticks, this is a complete meal.

In a large heavy soup pot or kettle combine all the ingredients except the hot pepper sauce and liquid smoke and bring the stock to a boil over moderately high heat. Simmer the mixture, covered, stirring occasionally, for 1 hour, or until the peas are soft, and discard the bay leaf and cloves. With a potato masher or heavy whisk mash the soup lightly to achieve the desired consistency or purée a portion of it in a food processor and stir the puréed mixture back into the soup. Stir in the hot pepper sauce, liquid smoke to taste if desired, and salt to taste. The soup keeps, covered and chilled, for several days. Serves 4 to 6.

P&B's Hints: It's easier to find and later fish out the bay leaf and cloves if you tie them in a small piece of cheesecloth. If you do happen to have ham stock you can eliminate the kielbasa and add 1 cup diced ham at the end instead. In place of the herbs we've used, substitute any others whose flavors you prefer.

LENTIL SOUP

Running a close second to split pea in the wintertime lunch sweepstakes was lentil soup, another byproduct of Sunday dinner's baked ham. The version that we grew up on was pretty simple: lentils, onion, and celery in a home-made ham stock. Our current version is more vegetable-rich and complex in flavor. This soup is very adaptable, so make whatever substitutions or additions suit your fancy (not everyone likes parsnips as much as we do). You may have noticed that we call for cilantro in a lot of our dishes. That's because we really love it—it's especially nice with this soup.

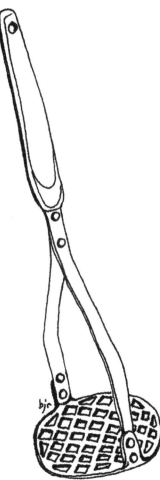

In a large heavy soup pot or kettle combine the ham stock, lentils, and chile, bring the stock to a boil over moderately high heat, and simmer the mixture, covered, stirring occasionally, for 20 minutes, or until the lentils are almost tender. Add all the remaining ingredients except the Worcestershire sauce and cilantro and simmer the mixture, covered, stirring occasionally, for 20 minutes, or until the lentils and vegetables are very soft. With a potato masher or heavy whisk mash the contents in the pot gently to obtain the desired consistency, somewhere between chunky and well blended. Stir in the Worcestershire sauce, cilantro, and salt and pepper to taste. The soup keeps, covered and chilled, for several days. Serves 8 to 10.

7 to 8 cups ham stock, chicken stock or broth, or a combination

1½ cups lentils, rinsed and picked over

a ½-inch piece of dried chipotle chile (optional)

1 cup finely diced celery, including the leaves

¾ cup chopped onion

1⅓ cups finely diced carrots

1 cup finely diced parsnips (optional)

¾ cup diced potato

½ cup finely diced green bell pepper

1 large garlic clove, minced

1 teaspoon dried thyme

1 teaspoon salt

1 cup diced ham or chopped kielbasa or ½ cup crisp-cooked crumbled bacon

Worcestershire sauce to taste

lots of minced cilantro or parsley

PROVENÇAL-STYLE FISH SOUP

¼ teaspoon crumbled saffron

2½ cups peeled and diced potato (about 1 pound)

1 cup well-washed finely chopped leek

1 cup diced celery

1 cup chopped onion

½ cup diced green bell pepper

½ cup diced fennel bulb (optional)

4 garlic cloves, minced

2 tablespoons olive oil

1 cup fruity white wine

5 cups fish stock or bottled clam juice

a 14-ounce can diced tomatoes with the juice

a 6-ounce can tomato sauce

½ teaspoon dried herbes de Provence, thyme, or oregano

a large pinch of sugar

1½ pounds mixed cubed fish or chopped shellfish

2 tablespoons minced parsley

crusty French bread as an accompaniment

In the corner of the Northeast where we lived, there were two opposing schools of thought on what constituted a proper clam chowder, and various family members had firmly staked-out positions on the subject. Grandma was adamant that the tomato-based Manhattan style (as opposed to the creamy New England style) was the only legitimate contender. To make her version, she would start by steaming buckets of the hard-shelled mollusks in a giant kettle and then grinding the shucked meat in a heavy, hand-cranked contraption that screwed onto the edge of her kitchen table. The briny steaming liquor formed the basis of the broth, to which she added chopped tomato, diced potato and celery, and garden herbs. A couple hours later we all sat down to a supper of fresh chowder and homemade bread. Any extra soup was packed into glass-lidded Mason jars to be trekked off to friends and neighbors. Our streamlined takeoff on Grandma's Manhattan-style chowder starts with clam broth and tomato and incorporates a variety of provençal-style flavorings. As with most soups we make, the proportions and ingredients called for are really just guidelines—so doctor the recipe to suit your taste. (If you're not fond of its anise flavor, leave the fennel out.) We like to serve the soup with crusty French bread to sop up every last drop of the broth.

In a small dish let the saffron soften in 2 tablespoons water until ready to use. In a saucepan cook the potato in boiling salted water until it is softened, drain and rinse it, and reserve it. In a heavy soup pot or kettle cook the leek, celery, onion, green pepper, fennel, and garlic in the oil over moderately low heat, stirring occasionally, until they are barely softened. Add the wine and cook the mixture over moderately high heat, stirring occasionally, until the wine is reduced by half. Add the fish stock, tomatoes, tomato sauce, saffron mixture, herbes de Provence, and sugar and simmer the mixture until the vegetables are fully softened. In a food processor purée ½ cup of the reserved potato with ½ cup of the soup mixture and stir the purée into the soup along with the remaining potato and the fish. Simmer the soup, occasionally stirring gently, until the fish is just cooked through and add the parsley and salt and pepper to taste. Serve the soup with the bread. Serves 6 to 8.

SALMON CHOWDER

As good as Grandma's Manhattan-style clam chowder was, if it came to a contest between it and the creamy New England-style chowder, we would vote for the latter every time. With Daddy on our side as well, Mother converted, and the creamy style became the norm in our house. It, too, involved the tedious steaming of clams, plus the steaming liquor had to be cooked down and then thickened with a butter and flour roux before the addition of "top milk" cream. Though delicious, Mother's chowder never made it into our kitchens—it was just too tedious to make. Because we missed its creamy comfort, however, we developed the following alternative, using bottled clam juice instead of homemade fish stock and low-fat dairy products instead of cream. Also, we had to admit that we really weren't crazy about the tough chewiness of clams and so we replaced the mollusks with salmon, adding delicacy and attractive touches of color.

¼ pound bacon (about 4 to 5 slices), cut into ¼-inch pieces

¾ cup thinly sliced celery

¾ cup well-washed, finely chopped leek

2 tablespoons flour

½ teaspoon dried thyme

1 cup chicken broth

1 cup bottled clam juice

1¾ cups peeled and diced potato (about ¾ pound potatoes)

¾ pound skinless salmon fillet, cut into ½-inch cubes

1 cup low-fat milk

½ cup fat-free half-and-half

2 tablespoons dry vermouth or Sherry (optional)

½ teaspoon Worcestershire sauce, or to taste (optional)

2 tablespoons minced parsley

In a large heavy saucepan cook the bacon over moderate heat, stirring, until it is crisp and transfer it with a slotted spoon to a small bowl. Pour off all but 2 tablespoons of the bacon fat in the pan, add the celery and leek, and cook them, stirring occasionally, until they are softened slightly. Sprinkle the mixture with the flour and thyme and cook it, stirring, for 2 minutes. Whisk in the broth and clam juice and cook the mixture, stirring, for 5 minutes, or until it is thickened. Add the potato and cook the mixture for 10 minutes, or until the potato is softened. With a potato masher or heavy whisk lightly mash the potato so some of it is broken up and some remains intact. Add the salmon and cook the mixture, occasionally stirring gently, for 3 minutes, or until the salmon is barely cooked through. Gently stir in the milk, half-and-half, vermouth, Worcestershire sauce, and salt and pepper to taste and cook the chowder for 1 minute, or until it is hot, but do not let it boil. Gently stir in the bacon and serve the chowder sprinkled with the parsley. Serves 4.

P&B's Hints: Bonnie also likes to serve the chowder topped with crisp bread crumbs. Pat likes a slightly Scandinavian take on the chowder, substituting 2 teaspoons minced fresh dill for the thyme.

EURO-STYLE STRING BEAN SOUP

3 cups chicken broth

1 pound fresh young green beans, rinsed, trimmed, and cut into ¾-inch pieces

1 large potato, peeled and cut into ½-inch cubes (about 1¼ cups)

1 cup chopped onion

1 teaspoon salt

2 tablespoons butter

2 tablespoons flour

2 cups low-fat milk

½ cup low-fat sour cream (or full-fat if you want to indulge)

1 tablespoon white vinegar or tarragon vinegar if you have it

In Grandma's day they were still universally known as string beans, not green beans, as we now more appealingly refer to the new-and-improved stringless vegetable that growers have developed since. If you are lucky enough to obtain fresh pole beans from a farmers market or—better yet—from your backyard garden, they will elevate this summer soup from simply delicious to out of this world. Grandma loved this soup, Mother loved this soup (we used to sneak small containers of it into the nursing home), and we love this soup. It harks back to Grandma's Middle European roots and remains a favorite, especially if Bonnie makes it, because she somehow has always had a knack for growing fabulous pole beans. We have done little to alter the original, apart from lowering the cholesterol count slightly with low-fat milk and sour cream and using chicken broth in place of water for added richness.

In a heavy soup pot or kettle combine the broth, beans, potato, onion, and salt and bring the broth to a boil over moderate heat. Reduce the heat and simmer the mixture, stirring occasionally, for 15 minutes, or until the beans are barely tender. Remove the pot from the heat and let the mixture cool slightly. In a saucepan melt the butter, add the flour, and cook the mixture over moderately low heat, stirring, until it is bubbly. Add the milk in a stream, whisking, and cook the mixture over moderate heat, stirring often, for 4 minutes, or until it is thickened and smooth. Add the milk mixture to the vegetable mixture, stirring gently until the mixture is well combined. In a small dish combine the sour cream and vinegar, stir the mixture into the soup, and add salt to taste. Cook the soup over low heat until it is heated through but do not let the soup boil as it can curdle. Serve the soup warm, at room temperature, or chilled. Serves 6 to 8.

P&B's Hints: We often add ½ cup chopped kielbasa or ham or ⅓ cup crumbled crisp-cooked bacon for protein-hungry appetites.

CHILE CORN SOUP

Because we have always loved fresh corn on the cob, we tend to get overly enthusiastic with our farm stand purchases. So, after eating our fill of butter-drenched ears and having still more corn on hand, we are constantly looking for ways to incorporate the excess into other dishes. We bypassed Grandma's route of canning or pickling—even though we loved her corn chowchow, it was just too much trouble to make. This Southwest-inspired cream soup has become a choice solution, its mellowness set off with a spark of chile. If you get a craving for this soup in the dead of winter, you can use frozen corn kernels, just don't expect it to taste quite as good.

In a large saucepan cook the onion and corn kernels in 1 tablespoon of the reserved bacon fat over moderate heat, stirring occasionally, until the onion is softened. Stir in the garlic, red pepper, cumin, and chile powder and cook the mixture, stirring occasionally, until the pepper is softened. Add the broth, creamed corn, and potato flakes and cook the mixture, stirring occasionally, until it is hot and thickened slightly. Transfer 1 cup of the mixture to a food processor or blender, purée it, and stir the purée into the soup mixture. Stir in the bacon, half-and-half, and cilantro and heat the soup, stirring occasionally, until it is hot but not boiling. The soup can also be served chilled. Serves 4.

½ cup minced onion

1 cup fresh corn kernels, cut from the cob

2 slices of bacon, cooked crisp, crumbled, and fat reserved

1 large garlic clove, minced

⅓ cup finely chopped red bell pepper

1 teaspoon ground cumin

¼ teaspoon chipotle chile powder

1 cup chicken broth

a 15-ounce can creamed corn

2 tablespoons mashed potato flakes

1 cup fat-free half-and-half

2 tablespoons minced cilantro

P&B's Hints: We often make a whole meal out of the soup by adding chopped cooked chicken or shrimp. For an extra kick, you can add minced fresh jalapeño with the red bell pepper or canned minced chiles with the cilantro.

DILLED CARROT SOUP

1 pound carrots, peeled and sliced very thin (about 2½ cups)

½ cup chopped onion or shallots

2 tablespoons butter or canola oil

1 cup peeled and finely diced potato (about 1 large potato)

3 cups chicken broth (not chicken stock)

½ cup fat-free half-and-half

a pinch of nutmeg

1 tablespoons minced dill, or to taste

½ teaspoon salt, or to taste

Every vegetable had some healthful attribute accorded it by our mother. She was a nurse, which gave her nutritional pronouncements a clout that was hard to challenge when we were mounting an argument to eliminate certain vegetables from required eating. Vegetable soups appeared regularly on the table, usually concocted from leftovers or what was on sale that week. We weren't crazy about Mother's "mixed" soups, as they always seemed to contain more undesirable vegetables, such as turnips, than acceptable ones. Perhaps because of their natural sweetness, carrots (they were supposed to be good for your eyes) fell into the acceptable category for all concerned. Maybe that is why we created this carrot-rich soup, which invariably pleases family and friends. Besides being delicious and healthy, it has the added virtues that it can be made ahead and is great either hot or cold.

In a saucepan cook the carrots and onion in the butter over moderate heat, stirring occasionally, until they are softened slightly. Add the potato and broth and simmer the mixture, covered, until the carrots are very soft (about 20 minutes). Let the mixture cool slightly and in a blender or food processor purée it in batches until it is smooth. Return the mixture to the pan, stir in the half-and-half, nutmeg, dill, and salt, and heat the soup until it is hot but not boiling. The soup can be stored, covered and chilled, for several days. Serves 4.

P&B's Hints: This recipe calls specifically for chicken broth rather than stock because if the soup is to be served cold and has been made with chicken stock it will tend to gel slightly instead of being smooth in texture. We occasionally vary the flavoring, using thyme or cilantro in place of dill, or we add 1 to 2 teaspoons curry powder with the butter to spice things up a touch.

HERBED ZUCCHINI SOUP

Somehow we never learned and always ended up planting way too much zucchini (doesn't everybody?). Like Grandma and Mother, we then faced the challenge of how to utilize that less-than-welcome abundance. One of our solutions is this delicious, fresh-tasting summer soup. It's perfect for a muggy August night—and almost as easy as turning on the air conditioner. Although we think of it as a cold soup, it is equally good served hot or at room temperature. By the way, fresh herbs really do make a big difference here, so it's worth the effort to try and get them.

In a large heavy saucepan combine the zucchini, onion, garlic, and broth, bring the broth to a boil over moderately high heat, and simmer the mixture for 15 minutes. Remove the pan from the heat, stir in the basil and minced tarragon, and let the mixture cool enough that it can be comfortably handled to purée. In a blender or food processor purée the soup in batches, transferring it to a bowl as it is puréed. Add salt to taste and, if necessary, add enough of the half-and-half to thin the soup to the desired consistency. Chill the soup, covered, for at least 2 hours and serve it cold, garnished with the tarragon sprigs. Serves 4 to 6.

3 medium zucchini, scrubbed, trimmed, and coarsely chopped (about 3½ cups)

1¼ cups chopped onion

1 large garlic clove, chopped

2½ cups chicken broth

2 teaspoons minced basil, or to taste

2 teaspoons minced tarragon, or to taste, plus sprigs for garnish

half-and-half or light cream if necessary

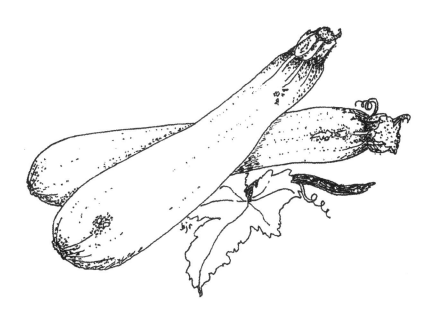

OLD-FASHIONED CREAM OF MUSHROOM SOUP

10 to 12 ounces mixed variety fresh mushrooms

2 small onions, peeled, one chopped and the other quartered and sliced thin

8 tablespoons butter

1 garlic clove, minced

1 teaspoon dried thyme

½ teaspoon freshly grated nutmeg

3 cups chicken stock or broth

4 tablespoons flour

1 cup fat-free half-and-half or light cream

½ teaspoon salt

2 tablespoons dry vermouth, Sherry, or Worcestershire sauce (optional)

minced parsley or cilantro for garnish

Grandma made a wonderful creamy rich mushroom soup. The problem was, it was pretty labor-intensive—not to mention artery-clogging. Because she had neither a blender or food processor, puréeing meant the mixture had to be "pressed through a sieve." So when canned cream of mushroom soup found its way into every pantry in America, Mother opted out of making Grandma's soup from scratch. Coming full circle, we now make something closer to Grandma's old-fashioned version. Try it some chilly day. Today's markets offer a broad selection of fresh mushrooms beyond the ubiquitous white button variety, thus giving us more interesting flavor options. We like to think, too, that we have made the soup a bit healthier by lightening the cream element without losing any of the soup's comforting richness.

Wipe clean the mushrooms, trim and discard any tough ends, and separate the caps from the stems. Slice half the caps finely, chop the other half, and mince all the stems. In a small saucepan cook the sliced caps and sliced onion in 2 tablespoons butter over moderate heat, stirring occasionally, until they are golden then remove the pan from the heat and reserve the mixture. In a medium saucepan cook the minced stems, chopped caps, chopped onion, and garlic in 2 tablespoons butter over moderate heat, stirring occasionally, until they are softened. Add the thyme and nutmeg and cook the mixture, stirring occasionally, for 2 minutes. Stir in the chicken stock and simmer the mixture, covered, for 20 minutes. Let the mixture cool slightly and purée it to the desired consistency in a food processor or with a hand immersion blender. In a large saucepan melt the remaining 4 tablespoons butter over moderately low heat, add the flour, and cook the mixture, stirring, until it begins to color. Add the half-and-half in a stream, whisking, and cook the mixture over moderate heat, stirring often, for 2 minutes, or until it is smooth and thickened. Whisk in the puréed mushroom mixture and cook the soup, stirring, until it is smooth and thickened. Stir in the reserved sliced mushrooms and onion, salt, and vermouth and serve the soup sprinkled with the parsley. Serves 4 to 6.

CHEATY QUICK CREAM OF MUSHROOM SOUP

If you love a rich creamy mushroom soup as much as we do but are in a real hurry as we often are, this version we've come up with is almost as good as the old-fashioned one and, in a pinch, even elegant enough to get by serving for a company meal.

In a large saucepan cook the mushroom caps, shallot, and garlic in the butter over moderate heat, stirring, until they are soft. Stir in the thyme, nutmeg, salt, canned soup, chicken broth, and half-and-half and cook the soup, stirring, until it is smooth and heated through but not boiling. Stir in the vermouth if desired and serve the soup sprinkled with the parsley. Serves 4 to 6.

4 ounces fresh shiitake mushrooms, caps only, thinly sliced (use stems for stock or discard)

1 shallot, halved and sliced thin

2 garlic clove, minced

2 tablespoon butter

2 teaspoons minced fresh thyme or ½ teaspoon dried

¼ teaspoon freshly grated nutmeg

¼ teaspoon salt

2 cans good quality cream of mushroom soup

1 can chicken broth or water

1 can fat-free half-and-half or light cream

2 tablespoons dry vermouth, Sherry, or 1 tablespoon Worcestershire sauce (optional)

minced parsley for garnish

SALAD

Lettuce in the supermarkets of our childhood usually meant either heads of crunchy romaine or crisp iceberg. Because no one in our family ever cared much for romaine, and iceberg was regarded mainly as a sandwich filler, most of the salads we grew up on were composed primarily of greens from the garden. These were augmented with a wealth of other garden vegetables: grated carrots, shredded cabbage, sliced cucumber, diced bell pepper, chopped cooked beets, and always tomatoes. Grandma was also fond of incorporating jellied things and pickled things into her salads because they made for light and refreshing eating on a steamy day in a house that lacked air conditioning. Although our houses are fully climate-controlled these days and our markets are stocked with a wonderful variety of salad greens year round, we still favor a number of Grandma's salad preparations—with our own modifications.

COLESLAW

1 medium cabbage, cored and finely shredded (about 10 to 12 cups)

2 large carrots, peeled and grated (about 1½ to 2 cups)

FOR THE DRESSING:
3 eggs

3 tablespoons sugar

⅔ cup half-and-half

3 tablespoons canola oil

1 tablespoon powdered mustard

2 teaspoons bottled grated horseradish

¼ teaspoon celery seed

¼ teaspoon dill seed

1 teaspoon salt, or to taste

1 teaspoon freshly ground pepper, or to taste

⅓ cup mild vinegar

Grandma made the absolute best coleslaw. It wasn't one of those finely chopped mixtures in a watery, semisweet dressing you find weeping away in the supermarket deli department. Hers involved soaking the shredded cabbage in ice water, grating fresh horseradish, and using heavy cream for the thick sauce. Mother's version used bottled salad dressing—good, but just not the sort of creamy, piquant salad that raised a humble picnic to gourmet status. We have found that soaking the cabbage is a step that produces little return for the time spent; and, with shredded cabbage mixtures available in most grocery stores, it is super easy to recreate an authentic, old-fashioned coleslaw that beats store-bought hands down. This dressing will be a tad lighter but equally luscious if the half-and-half you use is fat-free.

In a large serving bowl combine the cabbage and carrot. In a small bowl beat together the eggs, sugar, and half-and-half. In a small heavy saucepan whisk together the oil, mustard, horseradish, celery seed, dill seed, salt, and pepper and simmer the mixture, stirring occasionally, for 3 minutes. Gradually add the vinegar and then the egg mixture, stirring constantly, and cook the dressing, over moderately low heat, stirring often, for 5 minutes, or until it is thickened. Sample the dressing and adjust the flavorings and texture to suit your preferences (thin with water or more half-and-half if desired). Pour small amounts of the dressing over the cabbage mixture, fluffing and tossing the mixture with a large fork to keep it from compacting, until the slaw is coated with the desired amount of dressing, and chill the coleslaw, covered, until it is cold. Reserve any remaining dressing, covered and chilled, for later use. Toss the coleslaw lightly just before serving to redistribute any dressing that has settled to the bottom. The dressed coleslaw keeps, covered and chilled, for several days. Serves 10 to 12.

P&B's Hints: Once made, the dressing alone keeps for up to a week, covered and chilled, so you can prepare as much or as little cabbage/carrot mix as needed for immediate consumption, tossing it with the desired amount of reheated dressing. A far more dietetic version of the dressing can be made very successfully using fat-free half-and-half and replacing the 3 eggs with ¾ cup egg substitute and an amount of artificial sweetener equivalent to the 3 tablespoons sugar.

PICKLED CUCUMBER SALAD

As we look back, it seems that there weren't many things that Grandma couldn't pickle. Although her pickled pigs' feet still make us shudder, the cauliflower, green beans, beets, watermelon rind, and cucumbers were treats that everyone enjoyed. Most were "canned" for nibbling throughout the year, but her cucumber salad was a fresh summertime delight—lighter and tarter than the bread-and-butter pickles Grandma put up in jars. Salting the cucumber slices for a couple hours gives them a soft, silky texture and helps them absorb the sweetened vinegar.

Trim and discard ½ inch from the ends of each cucumber and with a vegetable peeler scrape off the skins lengthwise, leaving some rough strips of green (it's prettier that way). Slice the cucumbers crosswise no more than ¹⁄₁₆ inch thick, quarter the half onion lengthwise, and slice it crosswise as thin as possible. Layer the cucumber and onion slices in a shallow dish, sprinkling each layer lightly with some of the salt, and press a piece of plastic wrap directly on top of the mixture. Cover the plastic wrap with a flat plate that fits just inside the dish, weight the plate down with several heavy cans, and chill the cucumber mixture for 2 hours. In a small bowl stir the sugar into the vinegar until it is completely dissolved. Remove the cans and plate from the cucumber mixture and press hard on the cucumber mixture, draining off as much liquid as possible. Remove the plastic, add the vinegar mixture and dill, and toss the salad together well. Add more salt if needed. The salad will keep, covered and chilled, for up to one day. Serves 4 to 6.

6 medium Kirby (or pickling) cucumbers

a small Vidalia or other mild sweet onion, halved lengthwise with one half reserved for another use

1 teaspoon salt

1 tablespoon sugar

3 tablespoons rice-wine, cider, or white balsamic vinegar

1 tablespoon minced dill

RED POTATO SALAD

6 medium red-skinned potatoes (about 2 pounds), scrubbed and halved crosswise

½ teaspoon salt

1 cup thinly sliced celery

½ cup finely chopped Vidalia or other mild sweet onion

¼ cup snipped chives, garlic chives, or finely chopped scallion tops

3 hard-boiled eggs, coarsely chopped

2 tablespoons minced dill, parsley, tarragon, cilantro, or other fresh herbs *1 T dried*

1 cup mayonnaise

¼ cup sour cream

¼ cup sweet pickle relish

1 tablespoon Dijon-style mustard

1 tablespoon bottled grated horseradish

This is our favorite mayo-based potato salad. To slim it down some, we make it using fat-free sour cream and low-fat mayonnaise (the no-fat is a little too anorexic for this dish) and eliminate some of the egg yolk. It's still so good Grandma might not even notice the difference.

In a large saucepan combine the potatoes with cold water to cover and the salt, bring the water to a boil over moderately high heat, and cook the potatoes for 15 minutes, or until they are just tender. Drain the potatoes, rinse them with cold water, and drain them well. Cut the potatoes into ¾-inch pieces and in a large bowl combine them with the celery, onion, chives, egg, and herbs. In a small bowl combine the mayonnaise, sour cream, relish, mustard, and horseradish until the mixture is smooth, pour the mixture over the potato mixture, and fold the salad together gently until it is well combined. Add salt and pepper to taste and chill the salad, covered, for at least 1 hour or overnight. Serves 6.

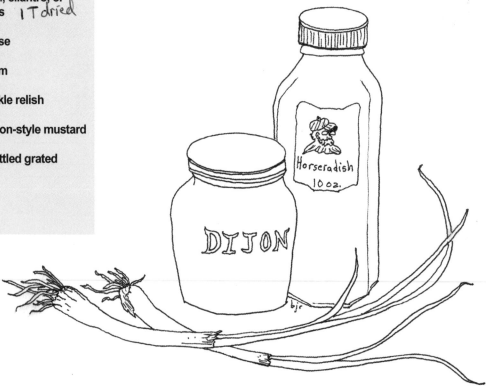

GERMANIC POTATO SALAD

Because Mother was allergic to mayonnaise, this was our family's regular potato salad. To this day we have done little to change its simple goodness. In keeping with Grandma's tradition-based approach, we serve the salad warm or at room temperature, but you can chill it if you prefer.

In a large saucepan combine the potatoes with cold water to cover and the salt, bring the water to a boil over moderately high heat, and cook the potatoes, for 15 minutes, or until they are just tender. Drain the potatoes in a colander, rinse them with cold water, and pat them dry. Peel the potatoes, quarter them, cutting lengthwise and crosswise, and cut them into ⅛- to ¼-inch slices. In a large bowl combine the potatoes gently with the onion. In a small bowl combine the vinegar, oil, broth, and garlic, pour the dressing over the potato mixture, and toss the salad together very gently. Add salt and pepper to taste and let the salad stand, covered, at room temperature, tossing it gently occasionally, for at least 45 minutes for the flavors to blend. Just before serving, fold in the bacon and parsley. Chill the salad, covered, if desired. Serves 6.

6 medium all-purpose potatoes (about 2¼ pounds), scrubbed and halved crosswise

½ teaspoon salt

½ medium mild sweet onion such as Vidalia, quartered and thinly sliced

3 tablespoons white vinegar or cider vinegar

4 tablespoons salad oil

4 tablespoons chicken broth

1 garlic clove, minced and mashed to a paste with ½ teaspoon salt, or use ½ teaspoon garlic salt

4 slices of bacon, chopped, cooked crisp, and drained

2 tablespoons minced parsley

P&B's Hints: The above procedure is designed for room temperature serving. If you like your potato salad warmer and slightly milder, cook the potatoes as indicated, then in a small nonreactive saucepan combine the onion, vinegar, oil, broth, and garlic and heat the mixture, stirring, until it is hot but not boiling. Pour the dressing over the warm potatoes and toss the salad together gently. Add salt and pepper to taste, the bacon, and the parsley and serve the salad at once.

TERRIFIC PACIFIC GELATIN SALAD

¾ cup boiling water

a 3-ounce package pineapple gelatin mix

1 tablespoon hoisin sauce

1 tablespoon soy sauce

1 teaspoon Asian sesame oil

1 teaspoon vinegar

2 drops hot pepper sauce

1 cup very cold water

1 carrot, shredded

1 scallion, minced

¾ cup finely shredded Napa or Savoy cabbage (bok choy and plain green cabbage are okay too)

2 tablespoons minced cilantro

1 teaspoon peeled and grated gingerroot

Grandma made a lot of aspics, and her pantry was never without a supply of that trusty standby, Knox Original Unflavored Gelatine (sic). Mother, on the other hand, made Jell-O. Her repertoire of jellied things included a selection of quivery vegetable salads as well as molded desserts with all manner of fresh or canned fruits stirred into them and a spurt of spray-can whipped cream on top. These preparations were fixtures at summertime neighborhood gatherings and church covered-dish suppers. Her carrot and pineapple combo was the version we saw most frequently and is an early ancestor of this Asian-accented salad.

In a heatproof 1-quart bowl add the boiling water to the gelatin mix and stir the mixture for a least 1 minute, or until the gelatin is completely dissolved. Whisk in the hoisin sauce, soy sauce, sesame oil, vinegar, and hot pepper sauce. Stir in the cold water and chill the mixture, loosely covered, stirring occasionally, until it is thickened but not hard-set. Stir in the carrot, scallion, cabbage, cilantro, and ginger and chill the salad, covered, for at least 2 hours, or until it is fully set. Serves 4 to 6.

P&B's Hints: With the addition of chopped cooked chicken breast or pork tenderloin, and dressed with a splash of soy sauce, this salad becomes a light, make-ahead summer meal. For additional crunch add ¼ cup drained and minced water chestnuts. If desired, serve the salad with mayonnaise flavored to taste with bottled hoisin, soy, or teriyaki sauce and extra minced cilantro.

MINTED PEA SALAD

Okay, we realize that this isn't a dish any male in three generations of our family would consider to be "guy food." Having said that, some version of this jellied salad mold has been a refreshingly cool and light family staple for decades of summers and is always a hit on the picnic table. Even confirmed vegetable haters will eat their peas this way, and we have yet to find any uneaten salad remaining on the plates of the male diners.

In a small nonreactive saucepan bring the broth (or 1 cup water) to a boil, stir in the gelatin mix and the jelly, stirring until both are completely dissolved. Stir in the vinegar, transfer the mixture to a medium-sized bowl, and chill it, loosely covered, stirring occasionally, until it is thickened but not hard-set. Stir in the mayonnaise and sour cream and gently fold in the peas, celery, scallion, and chopped mint. Spoon the mixture into a decorative mold or 6 individual molds or ramekins, lightly coated with cooking spray, and chill it, covered, for at least 2 hours. When ready to serve, dip the mold or molds briefly into a bowl of hot water and invert a serving dish on top of the mold. Turn the dish over and tap the mold to release the jellied salad. Surround the jellied salad with shredded romaine, iceberg lettuce, or your favorite salad greens and garnish it with mint sprigs. Serves 6.

1 cup chicken broth

a 3-ounce package lemon gelatin mix

4 tablespoons green mint jelly

2 tablespoons vinegar (whatever kind you like)

¼ cup mayonnaise

¼ cup sour cream

¾ cup frozen baby peas, thawed and drained well

½ cup finely chopped celery

2 tablespoons minced scallion (white and green parts)

2 tablespoons chopped mint leaves

salad greens

mint sprigs for garnish

P&B's Hints: If you don't want to go through the whole molding routine, simply spoon the gelatin mixture into a pretty glass bowl to chill and spoon portions of the jellied mixture out onto individual servings of salad greens. For the calorie-conscious, the salad can be made very successfully with sugar-free gelatin mix, reduced-fat mayonnaise, and fat-free sour cream.

TOMATO GELÉE SALAD

1 packet unflavored gelatin (¼ ounce)

¾ cup V-8 juice

2 tablespoons lemon juice

half a 10¾-ounce can undiluted tomato soup

½ cup minced celery

¼ cup minced green bell pepper

2 tablespoons minced scallion

1 tablespoon minced cilantro or basil

a few drops of hot pepper sauce (optional)

salad greens and dressing

We were all so accustomed to wonderful garden tomatoes that when the local crop was finished for the year we couldn't bring ourselves to add the mealy, flavorless off-season stock from the supermarket to our salads. Grandma's answer was to make tomato aspic, a practice we still follow today. Gradually her simple version evolved into our slightly more elaborate creation, which tides us over till juicy ripe tomatoes reappear in the markets and at farm stands. Aspic is an old-fashioned, fussy-sounding word, so, in order to appear more sophisticated, we call our preparation tomato gelée.

In a medium bowl sprinkle the gelatin over ¼ cup cold water and let it soften for 10 minutes. In a small nonreactive saucepan heat the V-8 over moderately low heat until it is hot and stir it into the gelatin mixture, stirring until the gelatin is completely dissolved. Whisk in the lemon juice and the half can of tomato soup (reserving the remaining half can for another use) and chill the mixture, loosely covered, stirring occasionally, until it is thickened but not hard-set. Stir in the celery, green pepper, scallion, cilantro, hot pepper sauce, and salt to taste then transfer the mixture to a serving dish and chill it, covered, for 2 hours, or until it is fully set. Spoon helpings of the gelée onto plates of salad greens and serve the salads with your favorite dressing. Serves 6.

P&B's Hints: Add other minced vegetables such as cucumber, radish, water chestnuts, or jícama. And, for a fancier presentation, chill the mixture in 6 ramekins or small decorative molds, lightly coated with cooking spray, dipping them briefly in a bowl of hot water to unmold. The recipe can also be doubled, chilled in a loaf pan, lightly coated with cooking spray, and served in slices.

TABBOULEH
(BULGUR WHEAT SALAD)

Grandma's concept of the Middle East fell somewhere between Scheherazade and Lawrence of Arabia, and the cookery of that part of the world was all but unknown to her. Although the tabbouleh that we make today would be a foreign dish, the concept behind it would not be, as the cold rice salads she employed throughout the summer as a means of using up garden tomatoes and herbs were similar in character. Had bulgur wheat been a readily available staple, we feel certain she would have embraced the grain and this Middle Eastern salad dish just as enthusiastically as we have.

In a large ceramic or glass bowl bring 1½ cups water, combined with the garlic, to a boil in the microwave. Stir in the bulgur and let the mixture stand, covered with plastic wrap, for 30 minutes for the water to be absorbed then drain off any unabsorbed water. Add the parsley, scallion, mint, soy sauce, lemon juice, oil, salt, and pepper to taste and toss the mixture until it is well combined. Add the tomato and toss the mixture together gently. Serve the salad at room temperature or chilled. Serves 6.

1½ tablespoons minced garlic

1 cup bulgur (cracked wheat), rinsed and drained well

⅓ cup chopped parsley

⅓ cup chopped scallion

¼ cup chopped mint leaves

2 tablespoons soy sauce

1½ tablespoons fresh lemon juice

2 teaspoons extra virgin olive oil

1 teaspoon salt, or to taste

1 cup seeded and chopped tomato

MACARONI VEGETABLE SALAD

2 cups macaroni, cooked al dente and cooled

2½ cups diced young zucchini (about 2 medium zucchini)

1½ cups diced red bell pepper (1 good-sized pepper)

1½ cups corn kernels

1 cup mayonnaise

½ cup plain yogurt

¼ cup half-and-half

2 tablespoon honey mustard

1 teaspoon grated lemon rind

1 teaspoon salt

freshly ground white pepper to taste

¼ cup (or to taste) minced dill, cilantro, basil, parsley, or other fresh herbs individually or in combination

salad greens

cherry tomatoes for garnish

We can't remember a time growing up when macaroni in some guise wasn't a mealtime fixture in our house. Mac 'n' cheese was the reigning regular, of course, but Mother also served the curly little pasta topped with spaghetti sauce, a "sloppy joe" mixture, or chili. Then, too, there was a seemingly endless stream of macaroni-based salad combinations, many involving canned tuna fish. On a hot summer day, cold cooked macaroni can be thrown together with a vast variety of ingredients that might be on hand and, voilà, you have a simple, one-dish meal that is appealing to virtually anyone. Although we've probably never made our macaroni salads the same way twice, this is a sample of what they often contain to serve as a guideline for your own experimenting. The use of low-fat mayo and fat-free dairy products will let you feel extra virtuous.

In a large salad bowl combine the macaroni, zucchini, red pepper, and corn. In a smaller bowl combine well the mayonnaise, yogurt, half-and-half, mustard, lemon juice, salt, and pepper and stir in the herbs. Add the dressing to the macaroni mixture, toss the salad until it is well combined, and chill it, covered, for at least 1 hour to allow the flavors to blend. Serve scoops of the macaroni salad on a bed of salad greens and garnished with cherry tomatoes. Serves 8 to 10 as a side dish.

P&B's Hints: To make the salad into a nonvegetarian meal-in-one dish, add 2 cups diced cooked ham steak (about 10 ounces) or diced cooked chicken.

MARINATED VEGETABLE MEDLEY

No garden produce ever went to waste in Grandma's hands, and, since her total freezer space was taken up by two trays of ice cubes, that meant everything was usually pickled or preserved. Long before three-bean salad became ubiquitous picnic fare, cold vinegar-marinated vegetables, either individually or in combination, were a staple summer "salad" in our house. We never managed to drum up much enthusiasm for the waxy-tasting canned green and yellow beans called for in usual three-bean recipe and have followed Grandma's lead in going for more freshness and variety in flavor. Though we tend to be purists in many cases, even if we had time for shucking fresh corn or cooking up dried black beans or chick-peas, the effort just doesn't pay off taste-wise in this instance. For these ingredients, the grocery store canned products work just fine.

1 cup fine granulated sugar

1 cup cider vinegar

½ cup olive oil

1 cup chopped red onion

1 cup finely chopped red bell pepper

2 cups green beans, trimmed, cut into ½-inch lengths, and blanched

a 15-ounce can corn kernels, drained

a 15-ounce can black beans, drained and rinsed

a 15-ounce can chick-peas, drained and rinsed

¼ cup minced cilantro or dill, or to taste

In a large ceramic or glass bowl combine the sugar and vinegar and warm the mixture in the microwave, stirring occasionally, until the sugar is dissolved. Add the oil, onion (blanched briefly if you want a milder taste), red pepper, green beans, corn, black beans, and chick-peas, combine the mixture well, and chill it, covered, for at least 2 hours or overnight. Stir in the cilantro and ladle out servings of the mixture with a slotted spoon. Serves 8 to 10.

P&B's Hints: Other vegetables we have found to work well in this marinated mixture include diced celery, diced blanched carrots, diced cucumber, diced yellow squash or zucchini, defrosted frozen baby peas, and canned red or white beans, drained and rinsed.

MEAT

America is a nation of steak eaters, and meat in this country has traditionally meant beef. We grew up with this mind-set and the general perception that beef was a manly protein compared to other meats and especially compared to chicken or fish. We like beef for sure, but these days we share an equal fondness for pork and lamb and even various kinds of game. We look more closely at the nutritional aspects of meat-eating than either Mother or Grandma did, conscious of things like fat grams and cholesterol, and consequently try to limit our intake in keeping with our more sedentary life styles. We also like to experiment with a whole range of meats, varying the cooking techniques and the accompanying embellishments. Slapping a steak on the grill or putting it under the oven broiler is a pretty straightforward exercise; so, rather than reinvent that wheel, we've included some of the other ways we like to cook beef—plus a variety of different meats as well.

BREW STEW
(BEEF AND BEER STEW)

4 slices of bacon, chopped

2 pounds beef chuck, cut into 2-inch pieces

2 tablespoons flour, plus additional for dusting

2 large onions, sliced

2 large garlic cloves, crushed and minced

2 tablespoons butter or cooking oil

a 12-ounce bottle dark or amber beer

1½ cups beef or chicken stock or broth

1 tablespoon brown mustard

1 tablespoon cider vinegar

1 tablespoon brown sugar

1 large bay leaf

3 tablespoons minced parsley

To Grandma, beer wasn't a beverage, it was a cooking ingredient. As such, following a Middle European tradition, the brew turned up in a variety of robust stews that were cold-weather standbys in our house. Although we don't share Grandma's imbibing inhibitions, we do make sure that enough of the six pack remains to cook up this Belgian carbonnade-style beef stew on a regular basis all winter. Grandma served her stews with homemade spaetzle, but we usually opt for the easier accompaniments of rice or noodles.

In a skillet cook the bacon over moderate heat until it is crisp and transfer it with a slotted spoon to paper towels to drain. Pour off and reserve the bacon fat, leaving 1 tablespoon fat in the skillet. Sprinkle the beef with salt and pepper and dust it with flour. In the skillet brown the beef in batches over moderately high heat, adding more of the reserved fat if necessary and transferring the beef as it is done to a flameproof casserole or Dutch oven. In the skillet cook the onions and garlic in the butter over moderately low heat, stirring, until they are softened slightly, add the 2 tablespoons flour, and cook the mixture, stirring, for 3 minutes. Stir in the beer, stock, mustard, vinegar, sugar, and bay leaf and simmer the stew, covered, stirring occasionally to prevent sticking, for 1½ hours, or until the meat is very tender. Discard the bay leaf and stir in the parsley and bacon. Serves 4 to 6.

P&B's Hints: Instead of simmering the stew on top of the stove, we generally prefer to put it in the oven at 225° F. to slow-cook overnight—it's even better that way! The stew is best made ahead and reheated, plus it freezes well.

AUSTRIAN BEEF STEW

This recipe harks back to Grandma's Austrian heritage, using a thrifty cut of meat that lends itself to long slow simmering. Bonnie favors the caraway in seed form while Pat prefers it ground, but we both love the make-ahead quality of the stew. The dish is especially popular with those "meat and potatoes" family members—here left unnamed—who could happily live out the remainder of their lives without eating another green vegetable.

In a large Dutch oven or heavy cooking pot brown the beef in the butter over moderately high heat. Add the onion, garlic, mushrooms, and caraway and cook the mixture, stirring often, for 3 minutes, or until the onions are golden and the mushrooms have released some of their juices. Add the stock and bay leaves and simmer the mixture, covered, stirring occasionally, for 1 hour. Add the potatoes and salt and simmer the stew, covered, stirring occasionally, for 20 minutes, or until the potatoes are cooked through. In a small bowl mix the flour with ⅓ cup water to form a thin smooth paste, stir the paste into the stew, and cook the stew over moderately high heat, stirring, until the sauce is thickened. Discard the bay leaves and stir in the Worcestershire sauce and salt and pepper to taste. Serves 6.

2 pounds stewing beef, cut into 1-inch cubes

2 tablespoons butter or cooking oil

2 medium onions, coarsely chopped

4 garlic cloves, coarsely chopped

8 ounces mushrooms, sliced

1 teaspoon caraway (seeds or ground)

1 cup beef, chicken, or vegetable stock or broth

2 large bay leaves

3 medium all-purpose potatoes, peeled and cut into 1-inch cubes just before adding

½ teaspoon salt

3 tablespoons flour

1 tablespoon Worcestershire sauce

P&B's Hints: For a complete meal-in-one, add 2 cups carrots, cut into 1-inch pieces, along with the stock. The stew taste even better made ahead and reheated, plus it can be frozen.

SOUTHWEST-STYLE GRILLED STEAK

1 cup loosely packed cilantro leaves

4 large garlic cloves, minced and mashed to a paste with 2 teaspoons salt

2 tablespoons chopped canned chipotles in adobo, or to taste

¼ cup full-flavored olive oil

¼ cup fresh lime juice

½ teaspoon grated lime rind

2 tablespoons ground cumin

1 tablespoon dry mustard

½ teaspoon ground allspice

½ teaspoon freshly ground pepper, or to taste

4 rib-eye steaks, each about 8 ounces (or other steaks of your choosing)

Real beef, as we called it, was a big deal in our house growing up. Because it was pricey, filet was a rarity on the table and roast beef, which Grandma served with Yorkshire pudding, was reserved for special occasions. When it came to everyday outdoor grilling, the choices were usually "other beef," such as hamburger and London broil/flank steak. Pretty much unadorned aside from a quick dose of salt and pepper, the meat was good in a beefy sort of way but never managed to generate much excitement. Although we now have a larger selection of beef to choose from and abundant availability, we still find that plain grilled steak can benefit from some embellishment. This is one of our favorite ways to liven it up. Maybe the Southwest-style spicing is a throwback to all those Lone Ranger episodes we listened to on the radio and the campfire meals from cowboy movies.

In a food processor combine all of the ingredients except the steaks and purée the mixture until it is a fairly thick paste. (This mixture is best made shortly before using but can be made up to 1 day in advance.) Spread the steaks on both sides with the paste and let them marinate, loosely covered and chilled, for 30 minutes to an hour. Grill the steaks over moderately hot coals or on a gas grill until they are well seared and cooked to the desired degree of doneness. Serves 4.

CREAMED CHIPPED BEEF AND CABBAGE

We're not sure if our father really liked the food in the Army or it was simply nostalgia for the days when creamed chipped beef (SOS as it was referred to in x-rated military slang) was a mess hall staple. Or maybe it was just that chipped beef was cheap and easy to store. Whatever the reason, the salty dried meat found its way to our dining table with startling regularity. Sometimes it was mixed with hard-boiled eggs in a cream sauce and served over toast for breakfast, or it might be combined with creamed cabbage and served with rice or mashed potatoes. Either way, Daddy loved it and it has remained a sentimental favorite. It's hard to find real "chipped" beef in the grocery store these days. And this isn't a totally bad thing, as the authentic, old-style product often had to be thoroughly rinsed in order to reduce the massive concentrations of salt used to preserve it. Even the jars of pressed, sliced, semi-dried beef that are sold today contain enough salt that little, if any, needs to be added to this recipe. Cello packets of wafer-thin dried beef are a good substitute if you can't find the real thing.

half a small head of cabbage, cored and coarsely chopped (about 4 cups)

3 tablespoons butter

3 tablespoons flour

2 teaspoons prepared Dijon-style mustard

2 cups skim milk

4 ounces "chipped" beef, rinsed, patted dry, and shredded

toast, steamed rice, or mashed potatoes as an accompaniment

In a saucepan combine the cabbage and 2 cups water and bring the water to a boil over moderately high heat. Simmer the cabbage, covered, for 10 minutes, or until it is softened, and drain it well in a colander. In the saucepan melt the butter over moderately low heat, stir in the flour, and cook the mixture, stirring, for 1 minute. Whisk in the mustard and milk and cook the mixture, stirring often, for 3 minutes, or until the sauce is thickened. Fold in the cabbage and shredded beef and serve the mixture over toast, steamed rice, or mashed potatoes. Serves 4.

P&B's Hints: The cooked chipped beef and cabbage mixture can be transferred to an ovenproof dish, cooled, and then stored, covered and chilled, for up to 2 days. Reheat in the microwave or moderate (350° F.) oven.

VEAL PAPRIKA

2 pounds stewing veal, cut into about 1-inch pieces

2 tablespoons mild Hungarian paprika

½ teaspoon sugar

1¼ cups chicken broth or water

2 medium onions, quartered and thinly sliced

12 ounces fresh mushrooms, cut into 1-inch pieces (or the canned equivalent)

1 tablespoon cornstarch dissolved in a little water or bits of roux (page 87)

1 cup fat-free sour cream

Veal paprika was one of Grandpa's favorite dishes, rivalling jellied pigs' feet. It was one of our favorites as well (but forget the pigs' feet). Learning to make it from Grandma was tricky, however, for as often as we might watch, her preparation was never exactly the same. Following in her footsteps, we have become confirmed experimenters, and this recipe is an amalgamation of "most often" scenarios. Though Grandma would frown on it, we have opted for healthiness over richness and use fat-free sour cream. Homemade spaetzle was Grandpa's favorite accompaniment, but we find the stew pairs well with noodles, rice, or mashed potatoes. See page 129 for our vegetarian version: Portobello Paprika.

In a large heavy saucepan or Dutch oven stir together the veal, paprika, and sugar over moderately high heat, until the veal is well coated and seared slightly. Stir in the broth and simmer the mixture, covered, stirring occasionally, for 1 hour. Add the onion and mushrooms and simmer the mixture, covered, stirring occasionally, for 30 minutes. Stir in the cornstarch mixture (or the bits of roux), a little at a time, and cook the stew, stirring often, until the sauce is thickened to the desired consistency. Remove the pan from the heat and stir in the sour cream. Serves 6.

MEAL-IN-ONE VEAL STEW

We generally prefer the more delicate flavor of veal to beef in our stews. Although Grandma's veal paprika is OUR favorite, occasionally friends and family (especially the kids) prefer a less "foreign" taste. For them, we often prepare this simple stew. It can be put together fairly quickly and then set to simmer or be made ahead and reheated. We serve the stew in large soup plates as a one-dish meal. If we have fresh herbs on hand, we like to add a sprinkling of minced basil, oregano, or thyme.

In a large nonreactive saucepan combine the veal, tomatoes with their juice, garlic, onion, and a large pinch of salt, bring the liquid to a boil over moderately high heat, and simmer the mixture, covered, for 1 hour. Add the celery and potatoes and simmer the mixture, covered, for 25 minutes, or until the vegetables are tender. Add salt and pepper to taste and thicken the sauce if desired with a little cornstarch dissolved in water. Serves 4.

1¼ pounds stewing veal, cut into 1-inch pieces

a 15-ounce can diced tomatoes with the juice

1 garlic clove, minced

2 medium onions, diced

3 celery stalks, cut into ¾-inch pieces

2 medium potatoes, peeled and cut into ¾-inch pieces

cornstarch for thickening

SUPER LAZY VEAL STEW

We love to come home at the end of a long wintry day to a nice comforting stew. Alas, we have no stay-at-home mother or grandmother there to whip it up and have it ready and waiting. So, when we haven't had the foresight to make something ahead and the simple acts of measuring ingredients and chopping vegetables just seem too much effort, this mindlessly easy recipe is where we turn. While the dish is simmering, you can boil up some pasta, throw together a simple salad, and then sit down with your feet up and start sipping the rest of that bottle of wine you opened for the stew.

In a large nonreactive saucepan combine the meat, salsa, and wine, bring the liquid to a boil over moderately high heat, and then simmer the mixture, covered, stirring occasionally, for 1 hour (45 minutes if using chicken thighs). Thicken the sauce if desired with a little cornstarch dissolved in water and stir in the cilantro. Serves 4 to 6.

1½ pounds stewing veal, pork, or boneless chicken thighs, cut into 1-inch pieces

a 16-ounce jar of your favorite mild salsa

¼ cup white wine

cornstarch for thickening

¼ cup minced cilantro

BLACK BEANS AND SAUSAGE WITH RICE

1 onion, finely chopped

½ cup diced green bell pepper

1 garlic clove, minced

2 teaspoons cooking oil

2 ounces Mexican-style chorizo (or substitute kielbasa or other favorite cooked sausage to taste), diced

2 teaspoon ground cumin, or to taste

a 15-ounce can black beans with the liquid

1 tablespoon ketchup

½ teaspoon Worcestershire sauce (optional)

2 tablespoons minced cilantro

ACCOMPANIMENTS: steamed rice, shredded iceberg lettuce, seeded and chopped tomato, diced avocado (optional but we'd never leave it out), grated Monterey Jack or other cheese, additional minced cilantro for garnish

During the hot and humid days of July and August Mother tried to make meals that involved turning on the stove as little as possible. Thus, the back-yard barbecue saw a lot of use and grilled hot dogs—accompanied by baked beans and a big salad of garden greens and tomatoes—made an appearance regularly on the supper table. Maybe because of this, for years we thought that the expression "dog days of summer" came into being because it was a time for grilling hot dogs outside. If there are children around these days, we will trot out the baked beans and franks and nostalgically down some ourselves. A beans 'n' franks and salad legacy has stuck with us in other ways, however, cropping up in the following Latin-accented preparation of black beans with chorizo. Served atop rice with shredded lettuce, chopped tomato, and avocado, it is a fast and easy complete meal summer or winter.

In a skillet cook the onion, green pepper, and garlic in the oil over moderate heat, stirring, until they are softened slightly. Add the sausage and cumin and cook the mixture, stirring, for 2 minutes. Add the black beans with their liquid, ketchup, Worcestershire sauce, and salt to taste and simmer the mixture, stirring occasionally, for a few minutes to blend the flavors. (The dish can be made ahead up to this point—even covered and chilled overnight—and reheated.) Stir in the 2 tablespoons cilantro and simmer the mixture until it is heated through. For each serving, spoon some of the black bean mixture over steamed rice and top it with some of the lettuce, tomato, avocado, cheese, and a sprinkle of cilantro. Serves 2 to 4.

P&B's Hints: A vegetarian version can be made by eliminating the sausage and adding other veggies such as corn kernels and diced summer squash. For a spicier version, replace all or part of the green pepper with a hotter chile pepper or add hot pepper sauce.

OLD-WORLD BOILED DINNER

The traditional New England boiled dinner, better known around St. Patrick's Day as corned beef and cabbage, was an occasional winter meal in our house. More often, however, our boiled dinners harked back to a place far removed from New England or Ireland. The savory sausages of Middle Europe—bratwurst, knockwurst, or kielbasa-style garlic sausage—were the meats that customarily found their way into Grandma's pot along with the familiar complement of vegetables. Cooking more quickly than corned beef, these wonderful old-world favorites make dinner a breeze and create, as a bonus, a delicious spicy soup stock.

If using bratwurst or knockwurst, prick each sausage in several places with a fork. If using kielbasa, cut it into 4-inch lengths. Tie the mixed pickling spice, cloves, and peppercorns in a square of cheesecloth or enclose them in a tea ball. In a large stewing pot or Dutch oven combine all the ingredients (except the mustard and bread, of course) with 3 cups water, bring the liquid to a boil, and then simmer the mixture for 30 minutes, or until the vegetables are tender. Remove and discard the spice mixture. Slice the sausage, divide it and the vegetables among shallow soup bowls, and add a little of the cooking stock to each bowl. (Reserve any remaining stock for soup.) Serve the boiled dinner with lots of Dijon mustard and crusty bread. Serves 4 to 6.

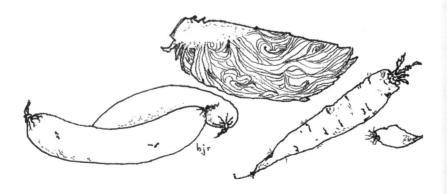

2 pounds knockwurst, bratwurst, kielbasa, or a combination

1 tablespoon mixed pickling spice or a combination of crushed bay leaf, mustard seed, and coriander seed

½ teaspoon whole cloves

½ teaspoon black peppercorns

2 cups chicken stock or broth

4 garlic cloves, peeled and chopped

1 medium green cabbage, cut into 6 wedges

3 medium potatoes, peeled and cut into 2-inch pieces

4 carrots, peeled and cut into 2-inch pieces, or ½ pound baby carrots

4 celery stalks, cut into 1½-inch pieces

2 medium onions, peeled and each cut into 4 wedges

Dijon-style mustard and crusty bread as accompaniments

SWINEBURGERS

1 cup crumbled rye bread
(about 2 crustless slices)

¼ cup milk

¾ pound cooked ham, finely
chopped in the food
processor (about 2 cups)

¾ pound ground pork, crumbled

1 small onion, minced

1 small Bosc pear, peeled,
cored, and finely chopped

1 egg, lightly beaten

1 tablespoon minced rosemary

1 teaspoon dry mustard

½ teaspoon garlic powder (or
1 garlic clove, minced and
mashed to a paste with the salt)

½ teaspoon salt

FOR THE SAUCE:
3 tablespoons vinegar,
preferably balsamic

½ cup lightly packed brown
sugar

¼ teaspoon dry mustard

It seems as if we had baked ham for dinner every other Sunday, and on more holidays than we can count. Not that this is a complaint—we do like ham—but, the ham had a way of mutating into a seemingly endless stream of dishes in the days following its initial appearance. Hot or cold and sliced or chopped or ground, the meat was the soul of versatility. Mother often used the ground ham to make patties, which were an offshoot of the deep-fried croquettes Grandma had made. Somewhere along the way, as we progressed from simple ham patties to a more elaborate version, we started calling our nouveau ham-and-pork patties "swineburgers"—a name that belies their lovely consistency and multilayered combination of flavors. They were no longer simply a pork patty, but "hamburger" was already taken, so they became swineburgers. Bonnie makes hers with seeded rye bread and Pat, seedless—your choice.

In a small bowl toss the bread with the milk until it is absorbed. In a larger bowl combine the ham, pork, onion, pear, egg, rosemary, the 1 teaspoon mustard, garlic, and salt. Add the bread mixture, combine the ingredients gently (we find using your hands works best) until they are well blended, and shape the mixture into 3-inch patties. In a nonstick skillet, lightly coated with cooking spray, cook the patties over moderate heat until they are browned on both sides and cooked through, transferring them to a heated serving dish as they are done. While the patties are cooking make the sauce: In a small nonreactive saucepan combine the vinegar, sugar, and the ¼ teaspoon mustard with ¼ cup water and cook the mixture over moderately high heat, stirring often, until the sauce is syrupy. Serve the swineburgers topped with the sauce. Makes about 10 burgers, serving 4 to 6.

P&B's Hints: The swineburgers also work well as small meatballs, having attended many a buffet dinner in that guise. They can be made ahead, can also be frozen, and reheat well in the microwave.

ROSEMARY APPLE SAUSAGE

Store-bought breakfast sausage, either in bulk or in brown-and-serve links, has an undeniably potent lure, but have you ever read the list of additives? Plus, the fat gram count is high enough to rival the national debt. Sausage doesn't have to be all bad for you, however, and making your own will take little time and effort to produce a truly tasty reward. Sausage can add incomparable flavor to stuffing, transform plain scrambled eggs into a brunch-time treat, or pair with polenta to make a light supper. Grandma's homemade sausage recipe, jotted down on a scrap of paper, was simple but a bit vague and yielded a huge batch of mild, dense forcemeat. Our updating has resulted in a more manageable quantity of lighter sausage but with an old-fashioned flavor that even Grandma would approve of. Plus these little patties smell SO good cooking.

In a large bowl combine all the ingredients (we find using your hands works best) until the mixture is well blended. Shape the mixture into sixteen 2-inch patties and in a large nonstick skillet, lightly coated with cooking spray, cook the patties in batches over moderately low heat for 6 to 8 minutes per side, or until they are nicely browned and cooked through. Makes 16 patties, serving 6 to 8 as a breakfast accompaniment.

1 pound lean ground pork

3 teaspoons minced fresh sage or 1 teaspoon crumbled dried

3 teaspoons minced fresh summer savory or 1 teaspoon dried

1½ teaspoons minced fresh rosemary or ½ teaspoon ground dried

½ teaspoon salt

½ teaspoon freshly ground pepper

1 Granny Smith or other tart cooking apple, peeled, cored, and grated

1 cup fresh bread crumbs

1 tablespoon maple syrup

P&B's Hints: The sausage freezes well and reheats quickly and easily in the microwave. If you want to make a simpler savory sausage, just eliminate the maple syrup and apple.

SPAGHETTI BOLOGNESE

1 pound ground pork or turkey

1 pound lean ground beef

1 tablespoon olive oil

1 cup minced onion

2 garlic cloves, minced

¼ cup minced celery

¼ cup grated carrot

1 teaspoon dried herbes de Provence or oregano

a 6-ounce can tomato paste

1 cup red wine

1 cup beef or chicken stock or broth

1 cup milk

a 28-ounce can diced tomatoes with the juice

a pinch of sugar

1 pound cooked spaghetti

Spaghetti (with a meaty red sauce) is a dish that almost everyone prepares somewhere along the way, even if it involves only opening a store-bought jar. Mother made a simple ground beef and onion/garlic combination enhanced with canned tomato sauce, which we ate over various kinds of packaged noodles from spaghetti to macaroni. The most embellishment it ever had was some dried oregano tossed in almost as an afterthought. We started out making her no-frills recipe until we discovered an important truth early in our single-life dating days: Spaghetti is great guy food, and cooking a mean spaghetti with meat sauce (followed by chocolate cake) was a sure way to win over a current love interest. Thus, over the years, our spaghetti dishes evolved into ever-more-elaborate concoctions. The sauces developed a life of their own during the cooking process as we added sausage, homemade stock, red wine, chopped mushrooms, and various herbs, simmering the mixture for hours and tasting as we went along until it had just the right flavor and texture. So, take this basic formula and do your own experimenting—it's hard to go wrong.

In a large heavy nonreactive saucepan or Dutch oven cook the pork and beef in the oil over moderate heat, breaking up the meat, until it is no longer pink. Add the onion, garlic, celery, carrot, and herbs and cook the mixture, stirring occasionally, until the onion is softened slightly. Stir in the tomato paste and when it its incorporated stir in the wine, stock, milk, tomatoes, and sugar and simmer the mixture, stirring occasionally to prevent sticking, for 1 hour, or until the flavors are well combined and the sauce is thickened. Serve the sauce over spaghetti noodles. Serves 6.

P&B's Hints: The sauce can be made ahead—it tastes even better reheated—and it freezes beautifully for a quick-thaw meal.

SWEDISH MEATBALLS

Meatballs to Grandma meant small round alternatives to meat loaf, covered with brown gravy and served over wide egg noodles. To Mother they meant meaty rounds the size of golf balls, served in a tomato sauce over spaghetti, much like a dish we might get in a basic red-sauce Italian restaurant. Our favorite meatballs, however, are a version that Bonnie developed with a nod to her husband's Scandinavian roots. Rather than employing the laborious pan-sautéing of Grandma's and Mother's versions, these are quickly done in the microwave. Make the meatballs inch-size and they will be the first thing to disappear from an cocktail party buffet. Or make them larger and serve them over egg noodles as an old-fashioned comfort-food family supper. For slightly lighter meatballs, replace the meatloaf mix with ground turkey or chicken.

¾ cup minced onion

1 tablespoon butter

1 teaspoon caraway seeds or ground caraway

1½ pounds meatloaf mix

2 cups soft bread crumbs, made from 3 to 4 slices of rye bread

2 eggs, beaten

2 tablespoons half-and-half

1 tablespoon Worcestershire sauce

1 teaspoon salt

½ teaspoon nutmeg

¼ cup minced parsley

FOR THE GRAVY:
3 tablespoons butter

4 tablespoons flour

1½ cups chicken broth

1½ teaspoons instant coffee granules

¾ teaspoon sugar

¾ teaspoon salt

⅓ cup sour cream

In a small skillet cook the onion in the 1 tablespoon butter with the caraway over moderately low heat, stirring, until it is soft. In a large bowl combine well the onion mixture with the meatloaf mix, bread crumbs, egg, half-and-half, Worcestershire sauce, salt, nutmeg, and parsley (we find using your hands works best). Shape the mixture into 1-inch balls and arrange the balls as close together as possible without touching in microwaveable dishes. In the microwave cook the meatballs in batches, covered with vented plastic wrap, for 3 minutes, or until they are cooked through. For the gravy, in a saucepan melt the 3 tablespoons butter, add the flour, and cook the mixture over moderately low heat, stirring, until it just begins to color. Whisk in the broth, coffee, sugar, and salt and cook the gravy mixture, stirring, until it is thick and smooth. Remove the pan from the heat, let the gravy cool slightly, and stir in the sour cream. In a serving dish combine the meatballs with the gravy. Makes about 80 hors-d'oeuvre meatballs or serves 4 to 6 as an entrée.

P&B's Hints: The meatballs can be made ahead, chilled covered, and reheated in the microwave for a party. They also freeze well either sauced or unsauced. We usually double the amount of gravy because it is so good and useful for saucing leftover meatloaf, beef, or chicken.

HAM STEAK WITH ORANGE CIDER SAUCE

2 tablespoons brown sugar

1 tablespoon flour

1 cup apple cider

¼ cup frozen orange juice concentrate, thawed

1 tablespoon balsamic or cider vinegar

1 tablespoon butter

1 teaspoon Dijon-style mustard

2 tablespoons golden raisins, softened in hot water if necessary and drained well

a 1-pound ham steak

Grandma's baked ham, essentially unadorned except for a clove-studded brown sugar crust, had a wonderful smoky richness. Not to diminish Grandma's cooking, but we suspect that old-fashioned curing methods had much to do with the peerless flavor and texture—a far cry from the insipid taste and water-logged slipperiness found in many of today's supermarket hams. With scant time to bake a whole ham (and little desire for a week's worth of leftovers), we most often seek out high quality bone-in ham steaks as a quick and satisfying alternative. To perk up their plainness, we like to serve them with this tart-sweet fruity sauce.

In a small nonreactive saucepan combine the sugar and flour and whisk in the cider, a little at a time, whisking until the sugar and flour are dissolved. Add the orange juice, vinegar, and butter and cook the mixture over moderate heat, stirring, until the sauce is thickened and smooth. Whisk in the mustard and stir in the raisins. You should have about 1½ cups sauce. In a large nonstick skillet, lightly coated with cooking spray, cook the ham steak over moderately high heat until it is lightly browned on both sides and heated through. Serve the ham, cut into serving portions and topped with the sauce. Serves 2 to 4.

P&B's Hints: This sauce also goes well with roast pork tenderloin, roast/rotisserie chicken, or roast duck. Without the raisins it can also be used as a basting sauce for grilling. The sauce can be made several days ahead and (minus the raisins) frozen as well. Bonnie also likes to use any leftover sauce on top of baked sweet potato or acorn squash.

CHINESE FOOD

In an effort to try and describe China to us and where it was located, Daddy explained that it was the place you'd end up if you dug down deep enough in our backyard and came out on the other side of the globe. This geography lesson was always amended with the admonition to eat everything on our plates because we were "more fortunate than the poor starving children in China." Sometimes when lima beans or liver (Bonnie and Pat's least favorite foods, respectively) were served, we were ready to head outside with our sandbox shovels so we could get the food to those starving children instead of us. Back then, Chinese food generally meant chow mein, chop suey, and fried rice. An Americanized version of soy sauce, which had recently appeared on the culinary scene, constituted the central flavoring that rendered a dish "Oriental." Although Mother dabbled in cooking with soy sauce, Grandma would have none of it. A generation later, Chinese food is widely recognized as one of the world's great cuisines and Chinatowns proliferate in many major cities. With the widespread availability of international produce, Chinese food has become a mainstay of our everyday eating in restaurants (or takeout ordering) and in our home cooking as well. Not only do we prepare specific Chinese dishes, but we also incorporate Asian ingredients and flavors in many of our more traditionally American recipes. If Grandma only knew what she missed out on!

SOY-BRAISED PORK

a 3-pound (or so) boneless fresh pork shoulder, butt, or picnic

½ cup soy sauce

2 tablespoons brown sugar dissolved in 2 cups water

¼ cup rice wine or dry Sherry

2 slices of peeled gingerroot about the size of a quarter

1 garlic clove, crushed and minced

2 large scallions, cut into 2-inch lengths

1 star anise (optional)

Although it lagged behind baked ham in frequency of appearance, pork roast turned up often on our Sunday dinner table—always accompanied by its sidekick, applesauce. Ham was the more versatile and economical choice (especially regarding leftovers), but we all secretly liked pork roast better, mainly because it had a rich brown gravy to pour over mashed potatoes or Grandma's spaetzle. We still love pork roast, but, as our taste buds have gone global, we now often prepare the meat in a Chinese manner known as red cooking. The pork is simmered to melting tenderness in an aromatic soy-infused broth and served either hot or cold, depending on the season or personal preference. Red-cooked pork also has made good leftovers on the rare occasion that we've had any left over.

In a heavy pot just large enough to hold it snuggly, combine the pork with cold water to cover it by 2 inches, bring the water to a boil, and boil the mixture for 5 minutes. Drain and rinse the pork and return it to the pot. Add the soy sauce, sugar-water mixture, rice wine, ginger, garlic, scallion, and star anise if desired and bring the liquid to a boil over moderately high heat. Simmer the mixture, covered, turning the pork over occasionally, for 3 hours, or until it is very tender. Transfer the pork to a cutting board and strain the cooking liquid into a bowl. Serve the pork hot or at room temperature, sliced and topped with some of the cooking liquid. Or serve the pork chilled, sliced and napped with some of the cooking liquid warmed slightly. Serves 8 to 10.

P&B's Hints: In summer we also like the red-cooked pork made into a jellied loaf. For this, chop the cooked pork and scatter it and ⅓ cup minced scallion in a 9- by 5-inch loaf pan, lined with 2 sheets of plastic wrap that overlap the sides and the ends of the pan by 3 inches. Strain the warm cooking liquid into a bowl, stir in a ¼-ounce packet of gelatin, and stir the mixture until the gelatin is dissolved. Pour the gelatin mixture over the pork mixture, distributing the solids evenly, and chill the mixture, covered, with the plastic wrap, until the gelatin is fully set (usually a couple hours). Oh, my gosh, is this loaf the Asian second cousin to Grandma's jellied pigs' feet??!!

STIR-FRIED PORK WITH VEGGIES AND CASHEWS

One of Mother's dinner staples consisted of cubed steak, a thrifty cut, sliced into thin strips and sautéed with peppers and onions and served over rice. For variety, an Asian effect was created by adding a sprinkling of that still fairly exotic condiment, soy sauce. The dish was an early forerunner of the Chinese-style stir-frys that we prepare today. A selection of Asian ingredients is now stocked in virtually every major supermarket, and stir-frying is an easy way to get dinner on the table with little time and effort. This recipe is one of our favorite stir-fry combinations, from which you can create your own variations. Other things we often include are shiitake mushrooms, fermented black beans, chili paste, and peanuts instead of cashews. Prepare and measure out all of the ingredients ahead of time, then, with just a few minutes of cooking, the dish is on the table.

In a bowl combine the cornstarch, soy sauce, and Sherry and toss the pork with the mixture until it is well coated. Heat a wok or heavy skillet over high heat until it is hot, add the sesame oil and 1 tablespoon of the canola oil, and swirl the wok to distribute the oils evenly. Add the red pepper, water chestnuts, and snow peas and stir-fry them for 2 minutes. Add the scallion, garlic, and gingerroot, stir-fry the mixture for 1 minute, and transfer it to a bowl. Heat the remaining tablespoon oil in the wok and in it stir-fry the pork mixture for 1 minute, or until it is no longer pink. Add the hoisin sauce and cashews and stir-fry the mixture until it is well combined. Add the vegetable mixture and stir-fry the dish until it is well combined and heated through. Serve the dish with steamed rice. Serves 4.

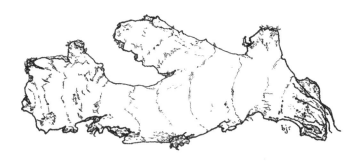

2 tablespoons cornstarch

2 tablespoons soy sauce

1 tablespoon rice wine or medium-dry Sherry

¾ pound pork, cut into 2- by ¼-inch matchstick strips

¼ teaspoon Asian sesame oil

2 tablespoons canola or peanut oil

¾ cup diced red bell pepper

½ cup diced water chestnuts

¾ cup snow peas or sugar snaps, cut into 1-inch lengths

3 tablespoons minced scallion

2 teaspoons minced garlic

2 teaspoons peeled and minced gingerroot

3 tablespoons hoisin sauce

½ cup salted roasted cashews

steamed rice as an accompaniment

SLOW COOKING

In the full circle of old becoming new, Slow Food is a culinary revival movement, gaining in popularity and gathering epicurean devotees. Grandma would have loved it—all of her food was "slow." Mother invested in the hottest gadget of her generation, the pressure cooker, to speed up the slow cooking process and later even dabbled with the newfangled Crock-pot, a plug-in replacement for the old-fashioned back burner. Employed in the working world, we could rarely muster up a whole lot of enthusiasm at day's end to start preparing the sort of full-blown home-cooked meal we might like to sit down to for dinner. The make-ahead, low-temperature oven-braising recipes that we've included here—slow-simmered lamb shanks (page 75), smothered pork chops in cider sauce (page 74), melting pot pork barbecue (page 73), and brew stew (page 56)—are a perfect solution. If you're a morning go-getter type, you can put one of these dishes together before heading off to work, allowing it to simmer all day. Or you can prepare it at night as we usually do, let it simmer in the oven as you sleep, refrigerate it in the morning, and have it ready to reheat for the evening's meal. It's hard to beat the unctuous flavor and incredible tenderness that results from this method of cooking. Most of the dishes freeze well, so with little extra effort you can make a double recipe, having one for dinner and a second ready in the freezer for an occasion when you are more pressed for time.

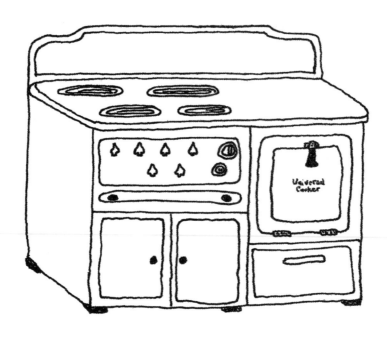

MELTING POT PORK BARBECUE

As Connecticut Yankees, "barbecue" in our childhood vocabulary meant grilling in the backyard. Our grilled steak or chicken might be smeared with a tomato-based sauce, but the results would never come close to what the term signified south of the Mason-Dixon line. Folks tend to get pretty partisan and passionate about exactly what constitutes the best or the most authentic barbecue, and in the face of all such controversy we probably stand out as heretics. We have yet to find a style we don't like, plus, when making our own, we generally break all the rules. We rarely have made the sauce the same way twice and tend to throw in international touches as the mood strikes us. When putting this book together, we assessed the various ways we have prepared barbecue over the years and quantified the following formula, which is a guideline for how we generally approach this dish.

1 medium to large onion, coarsely chopped

3 garlic cloves, finely chopped

2 teaspoons chipotle chile powder

2 tablespoons vegetable oil

3 tablespoons flour

2½ cups chicken broth

2 cups bottled ketchup

⅓ cup balsamic or cider vinegar

¼ cup Worcestershire sauce

¼ cup molasses

1 tablespoon hoisin sauce

1 teaspoon dry mustard

a 3-pound boneless pork butt, picnic, or sirloin roast, cut into several large chunks

In a large nonreactive saucepan cook the onion and garlic with the chile powder in the oil over moderately low heat, stirring, until they are softened slightly. Stir in the flour and cook the mixture, stirring, for 1 minute. Stir in the broth and cook the mixture, stirring, until it is thickened. Add the ketchup, vinegar, Worcestershire sauce, molasses, hoisin sauce, and mustard and heat the sauce, stirring, until it is well combined. At this point we transfer the sauce to either a crockery-style slow cooker or heavy casserole-style pot and add the pork. Cook the mixture in the slow cooker on low for 8 hours or overnight. Or cook the mixture in the casserole, covered, in a 225° F. oven for 8 hours or overnight. Transfer the pork to a cutting board and with 2 forks shred it. In a bowl combine the shredded meat with enough of the sauce to coat it well and add salt to taste. If you like a thicker sauce, reduce the sauce in a saucepan over high heat, stirring, until it is the desired consistency. Serve the pork hot or warm. Serves 8.

SMOTHERED PORK CHOPS IN CIDER SAUCE

6 good-sized sirloin pork chops

2 tablespoons flour, plus extra for dusting the chops

1 tablespoon cooking oil

2 medium onions, chopped

2 garlic cloves, chopped

1 cup apple cider

2 cups chicken stock or broth

1 cup peeled and chopped tart cooking apple such as Granny Smith

Every fall we looked forward to the local apples and fresh apple cider sold at roadside farm stands in our neighboring towns. The cider was rich and almost pulpy in texture and would get fizzy after a few days, unlike today's pasteurized product. Apple and pork make a great flavor combination, and homemade applesauce always accompanied both Grandma's and Mother's pork roasts. We continue the tradition in an adapted form with cider and pork chops. Slow-simmering the chops in cider results in meltingly tender meat and lots of slightly sweet, rich gravy for spooning over mashed potatoes, noodles, or rice. For this dish we prefer the texture of sirloin chops or cutlets over that of their pricier center-cut counterparts.

Sprinkle the pork chops with salt and pepper, dust them with flour, and in a heavy skillet brown them in the oil in batches over moderately high heat, transferring them as they are browned to a heavy flameproof casserole or Dutch oven. Add the onion and garlic to the skillet and cook them over moderately low heat, stirring, until they are softened slightly. Add the 2 tablespoons flour and cook the mixture, stirring, for 1 minute. Stir in the cider and stock, bring the sauce to a boil over moderately high heat, stirring, and cook it, stirring often, until it is thickened slightly. Add the apple, pour the sauce over the pork, and cook the mixture, covered, at a slow simmer on top of the stove, stirring occasionally, for 1½ hours, or until the pork is very tender, or slow-simmer it in a 225° F. oven for at least 6 hours or overnight. Serves 6.

SLOW-SIMMERED LAMB SHANKS

Lamb was available on a seasonal basis in Grandma's day, and roast leg of lamb was our family's traditional Easter Sunday dinner. The far cheaper lamb shanks were considered to be more pedestrian fare until their recent ascent into the realm of bistro chic. Though a whole roast leg has become a very occasional meal in our house, lamb shanks rank as one of our supper favorites; and, with their current fashionability, this dish now qualifies as casually elegant make-ahead company fare.

Preheat the oven to 225° F. Sprinkle the lamb shanks with salt and pepper and dust them with flour. In a large skillet brown the shanks on all sides in the oil over moderately high heat, transferring them as they are browned to a flameproof casserole or Dutch oven large enough to hold them in one layer if possible. Add the onion and garlic to the skillet and cook them over moderately low heat, stirring, until they are softened slightly. Add the 3 tablespoons flour and cook the mixture, stirring, for 1 minute. Stir in the wine, stock, and herbs, bring the liquid to a simmer, stirring, and simmer the mixture until it is thickened slightly. Pour the mixture over the lamb shanks and add extra stock or water if necessary so that the meat is submerged. Cover the casserole with the lid or tightly with foil and slow-simmer the lamb shanks in the oven for at least 8 hours or overnight. Serves 6.

6 lamb shanks

3 tablespoons flour, plus extra for dusting

1 tablespoon mild olive oil

2½ cups chopped onion

6 garlic cloves, chopped

1½ cups red wine

about 3 cups chicken or beef stock or broth or a mixture

several sprigs of fresh rosemary or 1 teaspoon herbes de Provence, tied in a piece of cheesecloth (optional)

P&B's Hints: This dish can be made ahead, covered and chilled, and then reheated in a 350° F. oven, stirring occasionally, for about 30 minutes. If you want a more gravy-like sauce, stir in bits of roux (page 87) or 1 tablespoon cornstarch dissolved in 3 tablespoons water and heat the sauce, stirring, until it is thickened.

INDIAN-SPICED GRILLED LAMB

about 2 pounds boneless butterflied leg of lamb

2 cups plain yogurt

1 garlic clove, chopped

1 teaspoon ground cardamom

1 teaspoon ground coriander

1 teaspoon ground cinnamon

1 teaspoon ground cumin

½ teaspoon ground ginger

½ teaspoon ground clove

2 teaspoons salt

several grinds of pepper

1 tablespoon minced fresh mint leaves or 1 teaspoon crumbled dried (optional)

One Father's Day during our teenage years we chipped in together and bought our father a hibachi grill. It was a featured item in an Asian import shop we frequented for purchases of incense, wind chimes, tie-dyed apparel, and other such essentials. The hibachi proved to be a great success as it was compact, easy to use and clean, and heated up more quickly and efficiently than the big backyard barbecue. It's arrival ushered in a new era of outdoor cooking for our family. Roast leg of lamb had always been a Sunday dinner favorite, and henceforth a boned and butterflied grilled leg came to rival it. Mother inserted small slivers of garlic into slits she made in the meat, and that, plus a liberal sprinkling of salt and pepper, was the extent of culinary embellishment. The lamb was always delicious. In later years, however, this Indian-style marinated and grilled lamb evolved into our current preparation of choice. Admittedly, the marinating procedure sounds rather implausible and the marinade itself looks pretty unappetizing, but the results are worth it. The yogurt produces a wonderfully tenderizing effect and the spice combination adds a delightful aromatic savoriness.

In a ceramic or glass dish large enough to hold the lamb comfortably combine the yogurt with all the remaining ingredients. Add the lamb, turning it several times so that it is well coated with the yogurt mixture, and let it marinate, covered with plastic wrap and chilled, for at least 4 hours or, preferably, overnight. Scrape off any excess marinade and grill the lamb over moderately hot heat, according to the directions for your grill, until it is cooked to the desired degree of doneness. Serves 6.

P&B's Hints: We peel and thinly slice a couple of extra garlic cloves and continue the family tradition of inserting slices of garlic into slits cut into the lamb; it is a savory addition we feel is well worth the effort. Do this before you put the meat in the yogurt mixture!

GRILLED LAMB CHOPS WITH GARLIC CREAM SAUCE

Both Grandma and Mother's legs of lamb were perfumed with garlic slivers inserted into tiny slits cut in the meat and by the bed of rosemary sprigs lining the roasting pan. We rarely have time to roast large chunks of meat, so when we serve lamb it is usually a more quickly prepared cut that can be grilled or broiled. The sauce in this recipe preserves the spirit of Grandma's lamb in a make-ahead manner. We buy jars of peeled garlic for ease in preparation and often double the sauce as it is also a nice topping for cooked chicken, poached fish, or steamed vegetables. Any remaining simmering liquid can be used to flavor soups, vegetable dishes, or pasta sauces.

40 large garlic cloves, peeled and left whole

2 shallots, peeled and sliced

2 cups fat-free half-and-half

2 large sprigs of rosemary

¼ teaspoon salt

12 small loin lamb chops

In a saucepan combine the garlic, shallots, half-and-half, rosemary, and salt, bring the liquid to a simmer, and gently simmer the mixture, covered, for 1 hour, or until the garlic is completely soft. Discard the rosemary, transfer the garlic and shallots with a slotted spoon to a food processor or blender, and process them, adding enough of the simmering liquid to achieve the desired consistency. (Makes about 2 cups garlic cream sauce.) Reserve any leftover liquid for another use. The sauce and leftover liquid can be stored, covered and chilled, for up to a week or frozen. Grill the lamb chops over moderately high heat according to the directions for your grill, or oven-broil them, to the desired degree of doneness and serve them napped with some of the sauce. Serves 6.

CHICKEN

After World War II, our father, like so many veterans with young families, set out with naïve exuberance to build a good life in an America awash in peacetime expansion opportunities. Eschewing the New York City literary and theater circuit of his youth, he somehow settled upon chicken farming in rural Pennsylvania. Mother and the babies went along. Two long years later, he packed us up and moved back to civilization—to the town where Mother was born (and died), where Grandma and Grandpa lived—to our hometown. We had a cozy little house close to town, and Mother had a most enviable collection of chicken recipes. Life was good. Accustomed, understandably, as she was to very, very fresh chicken, Mother soon established a working relationship with Mr. Rock who owned a chicken farm ten miles outside of town. Once a week his ancient gray station wagon would show up in our driveway with eggs, still warm from the henhouse, one stewing fowl, and (according to Mother's instructions) a roaster and a fryer or two broilers. Our father took an office job.

CHICKEN WITH ARTICHOKES AND SUN-DRIED TOMATOES

4 boneless chicken breast halves

1 tablespoon light olive oil

a 10-ounce package frozen artichoke hearts (or the equivalent canned)

2 ounces oil-packed sun-dried tomatoes, drained and cut into ¼-inch slices (about ⅓ cup)

2 tablespoons butter

2 tablespoons flour

½ teaspoon minced garlic or ¼ teaspoon garlic powder

½ teaspoon salt

1 teaspoon dried oregano

1 tablespoon minced fresh basil or 1 teaspoon dried

1 cup chicken stock or broth

¼ cup dry white wine

⅓ cup dry bread crumbs

2 tablespoons grated Parmesan

Taking our cue from an old family recipe for chicken fricassee that called for a cut-up chicken and a can of stewed tomatoes, we upgraded the ingredients to more exotic stuff than was in either Grandma's or Mother's provision pantry. The sun-dried tomatoes and artichoke hearts elevate this simple chicken preparation to a favorite company-quality dish. WARNING: Be sure not to substitute marinated artichoke hearts for the frozen or canned artichoke hearts—they are much too vinegary.

Cut each chicken breast half crosswise into 3 or 4 pieces and sprinkle the pieces with salt and pepper. In a large skillet sauté the chicken in the oil over moderate heat for 10 minutes, or until it is lightly browned on both sides and no longer pink inside, and transfer it to a 6- by 10-inch rectangular or 9-inch round baking dish. Cook the frozen artichokes according to the package directions, drain them well, and cut them into ½- by 1½-inch pieces. Scatter the artichokes and sun-dried tomatoes around the chicken in the baking dish. In a saucepan melt the butter, add the flour, and cook the mixture over moderately low heat, stirring, for 2 minutes. Stir in the garlic, salt, oregano, and basil and whisk in the stock and wine. Cook the mixture, stirring, for 4 minutes, or until it is thickened and smooth, and pour it over the chicken mixture. If the dish is to be served within a half hour, keep it, covered with foil, in the oven at 350° F. Just before serving, sprinkle the top with the bread crumbs and Parmesan and put the dish under the broiler until the crumbs are crisp and golden. Serves 4.

P&B's Hints: This dish can also be prepared ahead (minus the bread crumbs and Parmesan) and kept, covered and chilled. Reheat the mixture in the microwave, sprinkle the top with the crumbs and Parmesan, and crisp the top under the broiler. Or bake the chilled mixture, sprinkled with the crumbs and Parmesan, uncovered, in the oven at 350° F. for 45 minutes, or until it is heated through.

MULTINATIONAL COQ AU VIN

If you counted up all of the chicken dishes that Grandma, Mother, and the two of us have made over the years, they would easily feed a family of four for a decade or so. Suffice it to say that we are always experimenting with the very pliant, versatile bird to keep from getting bored. Grandma's staple chicken dish was a creamy fricasseed bird, Mother's was a more soupy Brunswick-style stew, and our current preparation of choice is an East meets West riff on the traditional French coq au vin.

In a large skillet cook the bacon over moderate heat, stirring, until it is crisp and transfer it with a slotted spoon to paper towels to drain. Pour off and reserve the bacon fat, leaving 1 tablespoon of it in the skillet. In the skillet sauté the chicken over moderately high heat until it is lightly browned and transfer it to a flameproof casserole or Dutch oven. In the skillet cook the onion, mushrooms, garlic, ginger, and five-spice over moderate heat, stirring and adding more of the reserved fat if necessary, until the onion is softened. Stir in the oyster sauce, soy sauce, chicken stock, wine, and bacon and bring the sauce to a boil. Pour the sauce over the chicken and cook the mixture, covered, over moderately low heat, stirring occasionally, for 1 hour, or until the chicken is very tender. Stir in the cornstarch mixture to thicken the sauce slightly and sprinkle the dish with the cilantro. Serves 4.

4 strips of thick-sliced bacon, cut crosswise into ½-inch pieces

8 skinless chicken thighs, lightly dusted with flour

1 large onion, chopped

1 cup sliced shiitake mushroom caps

2 garlic cloves, peeled and chopped

a 1-inch piece gingerroot, peeled and minced

1 teaspoon five-spice powder

2 tablespoons oyster sauce

1 tablespoon soy sauce

1½ cups chicken stock or broth

1½ cups Riesling or fruity dry white wine

2 teaspoons cornstarch dissolved in ¼ cup chicken broth or water

2 tablespoons minced cilantro

CHICKEN AND PEPPERS

2 green bell peppers

2 red bell peppers

1 yellow bell pepper

1 large mild onion (such as Vidalia), cut vertically into ½-inch slices

3 teaspoons minced fresh oregano or 1 teaspoon dried

3 teaspoons finely chopped fresh rosemary

3 tablespoons olive oil

1 large garlic clove, minced

½ teaspoon salt

4 large boneless chicken breast halves, lightly pounded between sheets of wax paper to a uniform thickness

1 cup shredded Gouda cheese

Our father was particularly fond of green peppers. He loved them stuffed, raw in salads, cooked with sausages or veal, but most of all, he liked Mother's chicken and peppers. A cut-up chicken would be oven-browned, then chunks of peppers and onions would be added to the pan to simmer in the fatty chicken drippings until everything was soft, brown, and greasy. Gosh it was good, but healthy…not. Our version calls for skinless, boneless chicken breasts, quickly sautéed, for a light, bright taste. This makes a very pretty and easy dish, as the pepper and onion mixture can be made ahead and reheated before topping with the chicken.

Remove and discard the stems and seeds from the peppers and slice the peppers into roughly 3- by 1-inch pieces. In a large heavy skillet cook the peppers and onion with the oregano and 1 teaspoon of the rosemary in 2 tablespoons of the oil over moderately high heat, stirring occasionally, for 10 minutes, or until they are softened and just starting to brown. Reduce the heat to very low, add the garlic and salt, and cook the mixture, stirring occasionally, for 3 minutes. Spread the mixture on a microwaveable, flameproof serving platter. Preheat the oven broiler. Sprinkle the chicken breasts with salt and pepper and the remaining 2 teaspoons rosemary. In the same skillet cook the chicken breasts in the remaining tablespoon oil over moderate heat for about 3 minutes on each side, or until they are lightly browned and no longer pink inside. Reheat the peppers, covered, in the microwave if necessary until they are hot, arrange the chicken breasts on the bed of peppers, and top each breast with ¼ cup of shredded cheese. Put the platter under the broiler about 5 inches from the heat for 3 minutes, or until the cheese is melted and starts to bubble. Serves 4.

CHICKEN AND BROCCOLI SOUFFLÉ

Grandma's soufflés—whether entrées, side dishes, or desserts—were peerless. But she was always in the kitchen fussing over the preparation and cooking time, and we always had to be ready when they were instead of the other way around. If you love soufflés but suffer a week of depression after seeing another perfect, puffy creation fall flat before it can reach the dining table, then this is the recipe for you. Although it uses leftover broccoli and chicken, it has an elegance that belies its humble beginnings and its kids-friendly taste makes it a great way to sneak more veggies into the little ones' diets.

Preheat the oven to 350° F. In a saucepan combine the stock, half-and-half, and tapioca and cook the mixture over moderately low heat, stirring often, for 5 minutes, or until the mixture is thickened. Remove the pan from the heat and stir in the cheese, mustard, seasoning, salt, and pepper, stirring until the cheese is completely melted. Transfer the mixture to a large bowl and fold in the chicken and broccoli. Let the mixture cool slightly and stir in the yolks, lightly beaten. In a bowl beat the whites until they hold stiff peaks, stir a small portion of the whites gently into the chicken mixture, and then gently fold in the remaining whites. Gently spoon the soufflé mixture into a 1¼-quart casserole or soufflé dish, lightly coated with cooking spray, and top the mixture with the bread crumbs. Spray the crumbs lightly with cooking spray, sprinkle them with the Parmesan, and bake the soufflé for 45 minutes, or until it is well puffed and springy to the touch. Serves 4.

½ cup chicken stock or broth

½ cup half-and-half

3 tablespoons minute tapioca

⅓ cup grated Gouda or Edam cheese

½ teaspoon Dijon-style mustard

¾ teaspoon Bell's Seasoning (or ¼ teaspoon each of dried thyme, rosemary, and sage)

½ teaspoon salt

⅛ teaspoon freshly ground pepper

1 cup minced cooked chicken

⅔ cup finely chopped cooked broccoli

3 eggs, yolks and whites separated

3 tablespoons dry bread crumbs

2 tablespoons grated Parmesan

P&B's Hints: Our recipe calls for Gouda or Edam cheese (because it gives a lovely depth of flavor), but you could also use the more widely available Monterey Jack or almost any other favorite grating cheese. Fat-free half-and-half and low-fat cheese can be substituted...if you must.

CREAMED CHICKEN CRÊPES

2 cups chopped cooked chicken

2 cups (a double recipe) white sauce (page 86)

6 beer-batter crêpes (adjacent page)

minced parsley, dill, or cilantro for garnish

When the roast chicken we often had for dinner was worked down to a scrappy skeleton, Grandma or Mother always managed to pick off a couple cups worth of small meat pieces before tossing the bones into the stock-pot. These little morsels usually turned up—thriftily and creatively—in some sort of croquette or creamed chicken dish, generally served over rice or noodles (frequently leftovers themselves) or toast. Though we don't carry thriftiness to the extreme that Grandma did, we find leftover cooked chicken in cream sauce to be one of the most satisfying of comfort foods. Using basic culinary building blocks (white sauce and crêpes), which we keep in the freezer, this dish can be put together speedily for a homey or company meal. When made with previously frozen sauce and crêpes, the dish can be prepared up to a day ahead and kept, covered and chilled. If made from scratch, the fully prepared dish can be frozen for later consumption.

In a bowl combine the cooked chicken with 1 cup of the white sauce. Divide the mixture among the crêpes, arranging it in a line across the center of each crêpe to within about 1½ inches of the edge. Fold those uncovered edges in over the filling, roll up the crêpes, and arrange them, seam side down, in a baking dish that holds them comfortably close together without crowding. Pour the remaining cup of sauce over the crêpes and cook the crêpes in a preheated 350° F. oven or, loosely covered with plastic wrap, in the microwave until they are heated through and the sauce is bubbling (times will vary depending on how cold the mixture was to start). Garnish the crêpes with a sprinkling of the herbs. Serves 6 as a first course or lunch entrée.

P&B's Hints: To the chicken and sauce mixture we often add chopped cooked mushrooms to taste or other green vegetables such as chopped cooked broccoli, asparagus, or spinach or cooked minced onion and garlic. If you're not up to making crêpes at all, the chicken can be combined with the white sauce and herbs to taste and served over toast, rice, or noodles.

BEER-BATTER CRÊPES

Grandma called them pancakes—not the fancy Gallic term crêpes—and her version descended directly from the simple egg/flour/milk Hungarian palacinta. They appeared at breakfast (filled with farmer cheese), at lunch or dinner (filled with creamed chicken), and as a dessert (filled with jam or cut-up strawberries in season and sprinkled with powdered sugar). We've slimmed down Grandma's version with fat-free dairy products and replaced the water she used with beer, adding both a lightness in texture and subtle mellowness in flavor. Although Grandma made it look easy, getting these simple pancakes to turn out just right can be a bit tricky until you get the hang of it—and we had a couple messy failures early on to prove it. One practice round with a nonstick skillet however will make you an expert in short order. The effort is worth it because these delicate pancakes are useful in so many ways and can be stored in the freezer, ready to create a dish impressive enough to make people think you spent all day in the kitchen.

3 eggs

½ cup fat-free half-and-half

½ cup fat-free milk

1 cup mild-flavored beer (if the crêpes are to be used for breakfast or dessert, substitute club soda or ginger ale)

1¾ cups all-purpose flour

¼ teaspoon salt

a big pinch of nutmeg

2 tablespoons flavorless vegetable oil

In a bowl whisk together the eggs and whisk in the half-and-half, milk, and beer. Whisk in the flour, a little at a time, the salt, nutmeg, and oil and whisk the mixture until it is well combined and smooth. Let the batter stand, covered and chilled, for 1 hour. Stir the batter to make sure it is well blended before cooking. Lightly coat a 9- to 10-inch nonstick skillet with cooking spray and heat it over moderate heat until it is hot but not smoking. Add a scant ⅓ cup of the batter and very quickly tilt and rotate the skillet so that the batter covers the bottom of the skillet in an even thin layer. Cook the crêpe for 1 minute, or until the underside is lightly golden (lift the edge with a non-metal spatula to check), flip it over, and cook it for about 30 seconds, or until the other side is golden. Slide the crêpe onto a plate. The crêpe should be soft and pliable, not stiff and crisp. Continue to make crêpes with the remaining batter in the same manner, stacking them on the plate separated with squares of wax paper to prevent them from sticking together. Makes about sixteen 8-inch crêpes.

P&B's Hints: The crêpes will keep, covered with plastic wrap and chilled, for up to several days and they also freeze well.

WHITE SAUCE

2 tablespoons butter

1 to 2 tablespoons finely minced scallion (white part), shallot, or onion

2 tablespoons flour

1 cup milk, warmed

¼ teaspoon salt, or to taste

a pinch of nutmeg (optional)

a pinch of white pepper (optional)

White sauce, cream sauce, or béchamel as it is more classically referred to, is the heart and soul of comfort food. Its flavor neutrality, its mellowing capacity, and its adaptability all make it the central component in a long list of easy-to-eat dishes. The ingredients—flour, butter, and milk—are kitchen staples, and some variation of this very basic recipe can be found in any kitchen primer. It was one of the first things Mother taught us to make, and we are rarely without a supply of it tucked away in the freezer for a quick comfort fix. The version we make most often is of medium-thick consistency and flavored with a hint of onion, but it can be made thicker or thinner as you choose by adding more or less milk. We usually use fat-free milk or half-and-half or a combination of both. The cholesterol-phobic can also substitute a light cooking oil such as canola for the butter, yielding a slightly thinner, blander sauce.

In a saucepan melt the butter, add the scallion, and cook the mixture over moderately low heat, stirring, for 1 minute. Stir in the flour and cook the mixture, stirring, for 2 minutes. Add the milk in a stream, whisking, whisk in the salt, nutmeg, and pepper, and cook the sauce, stirring often, for 5 minutes, or until it is thickened and smooth. Makes about 1 cup.

P&B's Hints: We also often add 1 teaspoon curry powder or smoked paprika to the butter with the scallion. For a cheesy sauce stir in up to ¾ cup grated Gruyère, Cheddar, or Monterey Jack. The sauce can easily be doubled or tripled and keeps, covered and chilled, for a few days and also freezes well.

ROUX (SAUCE THICKENER)

Beurre manié (kneaded butter), also known as roux, is a handy mixture of flour and softened butter, bits of which can be stirred into a sauce or gravy to thicken it. This method of thickening produces a sauce with a less pasty taste than frequently occurs when a sauce is thickened with cornstarch. Roux can also serve as a base for sauce-making. We feel that no refrigerator or freezer should be without it.

2 sticks (1 cup) butter, softened

1 cup flour

In a bowl cream together the butter and flour until they are fully blended together. Store the roux, well covered, in the refrigerator or, well wrapped, in the freezer. We often pack the roux in ice cube trays so that small amounts of it can be frozen, individually wrapped, for easy removal and use as needed.

To make **QUICK WHITE SAUCE**: In a 2-cup glass bowl or measuring cup microwave 1 cup milk on high until just before it is boiling (watch it closely). Whisk in 2 tablespoons roux and microwave the mixture for 1 minute, stirring it halfway through and again at the end. Add salt and pepper to taste. Makes about 1 cup sauce.

QUICKIE CHICKIE PAELLA

1½ pounds skinless boneless chicken thighs, cut into 1½-inch pieces

2 tablespoons olive oil

6 ounces Spanish chorizo, linguiça, andouille, or other spicy sausage, cut into ¼-inch slices

1 large onion, chopped (about 1½ cups)

1 red bell pepper, chopped (about 1 cup)

3 garlic cloves, minced

¼ teaspoon turmeric

½ teaspoon mild smoked Spanish paprika

½ teaspoon salt

2 cups medium-grain rice

a 14-ounce can diced tomatoes with the juice

¼ cup white wine

½ teaspoon crumbled saffron threads softened in 3 cups chicken broth

1 cup thawed frozen baby peas

3 tablespoons minced cilantro or parsley

Among the ways Mother managed to stretch a chicken into serving more people than it normally would was to cook it, cut up and combined with rice, peas, and diced carrots, in a slightly soupy white sauce. The result was a one-dish meal that was the epitome of economy-minded comfort food. We later learned that many cuisines around the world feature some version of a chicken with rice combination, and we quickly became fans of the spicier, more enticing Latin American arroz con pollo and Spanish paella. This dish borrows from both those preparations and has brought a wider world to our childhood comfort food.

In a very large ovenproof skillet or Dutch oven (or paella pan, if you have one) sauté the chicken in 1 tablespoon of the oil over moderately high heat until it is lightly browned and transfer it to a bowl. Add the sausage to the skillet, sauté it until it is lightly browned, and transfer it to the bowl. Preheat the oven to 375° F. Add the remaining tablespoon oil to the skillet and in it cook the onion, red pepper, and garlic with the turmeric, paprika, and salt over moderate heat, stirring, until they are softened slightly. Add the rice, stirring until it is well coated. Add the tomatoes with their juices, the wine, and the broth mixture, stir in the chicken and sausage, and bring the liquid to a boil. Transfer the skillet to the oven and cook the mixture, covered with foil, for 20 minutes, or until the liquid is evaporated and the rice is al dente. Stir in the peas and sprinkle the cilantro over the paella. Serves 6 to 8.

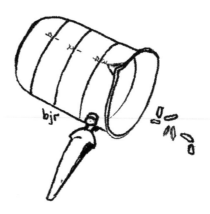

CHICKEN SCRAPPLE

Cornmeal—yellow, not white—was almost as common an ingredient as flour in Grandma's and Mother's kitchens and its warm sweet nuttiness lives on as one of our fondest taste memories. We, too, always have a supply of it on hand and have found that cooked cornmeal is a great base for using up leftover turkey, chicken, pork, or sausage. Our version of "scrapple" is a takeoff on the traditional Pennsylvania Dutch pork specialty. Pat likes it topped with salsa, while husband Bill swears by ketchup. Bonnie prefers it plain, and husband Wes—well, he is still making up his mind about the idea of eating scrapple at all.

In a bowl stir together the cornmeal and 2¾ cups of the stock. In a large heavy saucepan or Dutch oven cook the onion, garlic, and thyme in the 2 teaspoons oil over moderately low heat until the onion is softened slightly. Add the remaining 1¾ cups stock and bring the liquid to a simmer. Stir the cornmeal mixture to recombine it, pour it into the stock mixture, stirring to prevent lumping, and simmer the mixture, stirring often, until it is thickened. Add the chicken, salt, and pepper and simmer the mixture, stirring often to prevent sticking and burning, until it is very stiff in texture. Transfer the mixture to a 9- by 5-inch loaf pan, spreading it evenly, let it cool, and chill it, covered, overnight. In a skillet fry slices of the scrapple, lightly dusted with flour if desired, in the additional oil over moderately high heat until heated through and lightly browned on both sides. Serves 6 to 8.

1½ cups cornmeal, preferably yellow because the white tends to look unappetizingly muddy in this dish

4½ cups chicken stock or broth

½ cup minced onion

1 garlic clove, crushed and minced

½ teaspoon dried thyme

2 teaspoons cooking oil or butter, plus additional for frying the scrapple

2 cups minced cooked chicken or turkey

½ teaspoon salt, or to taste

white pepper to taste

P&B's Hints: If desired, add minced red or green pepper, cooking it with the onion mixture. Or add cooked corn kernels with the cornmeal. Scrapple slices can be sprinkled with grated cheese and browned under the broiler. We have also found the fried scrapple slices are delicious topped with a mushroom cream sauce. The scrapple mixture can also be served like a main dish polenta—just cook it to a lesser degree of stiffness and spoon it out. For more polenta preparations, see page 147.

CHINESE CHICKEN DUMPLINGS

FOR THE SAUCE:
3 tablespoons soy sauce

3 tablespoons mirin (Japanese sweetened rice wine)

1 tablespoon chicken broth

1 teaspoon Asian sesame oil

FOR THE DUMPLINGS:
1 egg white

1 teaspoon cornstarch

½ teaspoon sugar

1 tablespoon soy sauce

1 teaspoon Asian sesame oil

2 teaspoons peeled and minced gingerroot

1 garlic clove, minced

¼ cup minced scallion

¼ cup minced water chestnuts

¼ cup minced shiitake mushroom caps

½ pound ground chicken, turkey, or pork

2 teaspoons vegetable oil

a 12-ounce package wonton wrappers

minced cilantro to taste

What Grandma called dumplings and what the Chinese call dumplings are worlds apart. Hers were golf-ball-size lumps of bready dough, which were usually poached in water or broth for homey specialties such as chicken 'n' dumplings or other stewlike dishes. Theirs are a variety of dim sum or street food, consisting of a thin dough wrapper surrounding some savory filling. As we've strayed from Grandma's heavier, richer food, our concept of chicken 'n' dumplings now favors the dim sum concept. A big soup plate of these morsels, liberally doused in soy sauce, is a current favorite light lunch. We tend to encase all sorts of things in wonton wrappers—now available in most supermarkets—and, in endless variations on this recipe, we tend to incorporate leftover bits of this and that in the refrigerator. Grandma might not favor our dumplings over hers, but she would surely approve of them as a creative way to use up leftovers.

Make the sauce: In a bowl combine all the sauce ingredients and reserve the mixture, covered and chilled, for up to a week. Make the dumplings: In a bowl beat the egg white lightly with the cornstarch and stir in the sugar, soy sauce, sesame oil, ginger, garlic, and scallion. Add the water chestnuts, mushrooms, and chicken and combine the mixture, tossing it together lightly (we find using your hands works best), until it is well combined but not mashed together. In a skillet or wok cook the mixture in the vegetable oil over moderately high heat, breaking it apart into small bits, until the chicken is no longer pink. Transfer the mixture to a bowl and let it cool slightly. (The mixture can be made up to a day ahead and kept, covered and chilled.) Place a scant tablespoon of the mixture on one half of each wonton wrapper to within ¼ inch of the edges, moisten the edges of the wrapper with water, and fold the wrapper over the filling, pressing the edges together firmly with the tines of a fork to seal them. Arrange the dumplings on a plate, separating layers of them with sheets of wax paper until ready to cook. In a large skillet heat about an inch of water to simmering, add a layer of dumplings, nudging them lightly so that they don't stick together, and poach them, covered, for about 5 minutes, or until the wrappers are translucent and the filling is heated through. Transfer the dumplings with a slotted spoon to soup plates, drizzle them with the reserved sauce, and sprinkle them with the cilantro. Makes about 32 dumplings.

CHICKEN CAESAR SALAD WITH PEAR

Grandma's chicken salad, a summer dish she concocted to use up leftover pieces of cooked chicken too small for sandwich slices, could have been called Caesar salad for its flavor resemblance to the reputed creation of chef Caesar Cardini in the 1920s. Her creamy dressing was deliciously rich and also time-consuming to prepare—plus it included a raw egg, which in those days was not perceived to be as potentially health-threatening as it is today. If time permits, we may whip up a batch of Caesar-style dressing (minus any raw egg) from scratch, but more often than not we resort to a good-quality store-bought product. This dressed-up version of what Grandma made is Bonnie's favorite chicken salad.

In a large bowl toss together the chicken, celery, scallion, pear, cheese, dressing, and salt and pepper to taste and mound the salad on a bed of lettuce. Serves 4 to 6.

4 cups chopped cooked chicken breast

1¾ cups thinly sliced celery

1 large scallion, thinly sliced

2 medium Bosc pears, peeled, cored, and cut into ½-inch cubes

½ cup finely diced Pecorino Romano cheese

⅓ cup creamy homemade or bottled Caesar-style salad dressing, or to taste

shredded romaine or iceberg lettuce

P&B's Hints: If you want to make a Caesar-style dressing from scratch, here's one version: Mince and mash 1 large garlic clove to a paste with ½ teaspoon salt. In a food processor blend the paste with ¼ cup olive oil, ¼ cup mayonnaise, ¼ cup grated Parmesan, 2 tablespoons lemon juice, 2 tablespoons heavy cream, ¼ teaspoon Worcestershire sauce, anchovy paste to taste if desired, and a pinch of sugar. Makes about ¾ cup.

CHICKEN SALAD WITH GRAPES AND BLUE CHEESE

½ cup mayonnaise

¼ cup homemade or bottled blue cheese salad dressing

2 tablespoons milk

4 cups chopped cooked chicken breast

1¾ cups thinly sliced celery

1½ cups seedless grapes, sliced in half

¾ cup raisins

¾ cup pistachios or coarsely chopped pecans

1 scallion, thinly sliced

½ cup crumbled blue cheese

shredded romaine or iceberg lettuce

If Bonnie's husband, Wes, has anything to say about it, leftover cooked chicken in their house goes into this, his favorite chicken salad. And Stilton would be the blue cheese of choice.

In a small bowl combine the mayonnaise, salad dressing, and milk. In a large bowl combine the chicken, celery, grapes, raisins, nuts, and scallion and add the mayonnaise mixture, and blue cheese. Toss the salad together lightly, adding salt and pepper to taste, until it is well combined and mound it on a bed of lettuce. Serves 4 to 6.

P&B's Hints: You will certainly hear no complaints too if you serve the salad with fresh hot biscuits, rolls, or crusty French bread for spreading any extra blue cheese.

ASIAN CHICKEN SALAD GELÉE

Of all the summertime dishes that Grandma made, Grandpa's favorite was her jellied pigs' feet. Our father liked the dish too, so this creation appeared on our family's dining table as well. We, on the other hand, found this homey, old-world specialty totally revolting. First of all, the name sounded downright awful and the color was a thoroughly unappetizing murky gray. Then, if we somehow got beyond that, the greasy-tasting gelatin with its hard nuggets of meat and gristly cartilage was enough to have us trade off almost any treat for a reprieve from eating this "delicacy." The refreshing coolness and the make-ahead appeal of molded gelatin dishes, however, saved this legacy from total extinction and inspired the following light, Asian-accented preparation. Slices of the molded salad arranged on a bed of lettuce make a nice variety item for a summer buffet.

3 envelopes (¼ ounce each) unflavored gelatin

3 cups chicken broth

1 tablespoon soy sauce

1½ teaspoons hot Asian sesame oil (or ¼ teaspoon hot sauce combined with 1½ teaspoons regular Asian sesame oil)

½ teaspoon salt, or to taste

1½ cups chopped cooked chicken

2 celery stalks, finely chopped

½ red bell pepper, finely chopped

2 to 3 radishes, minced (or 6 to 8 water chestnuts, minced)

1 large scallion, minced

¼ cup packed cilantro leaves, minced

In a small bowl sprinkle the gelatin over 1 cup of the broth and let it soften for 10 minutes. In a saucepan heat the remaining 2 cups broth with the soy sauce, sesame oil, and salt until it is hot, add the gelatin mixture, and stir the mixture until the gelatin is completely dissolved. Transfer the mixture to a bowl, chill it, loosely covered, until it is thickened slightly, and stir in the remaining ingredients. For later easy unmolding and convenient serving slices, transfer the mixture to a loaf pan, lightly coated with cooking spray and lined with a large enough piece of plastic wrap to allow for overlapping the top and keeping the gelatin mixture covered. Chill the gelatin salad, covered, until it is firm. Serves 6.

P&B's Hints: The gelatin mixture can simply be chilled, covered, in the mixing bowl and spooned out with an ice-cream scoop onto a bed of salad greens for individual servings. Serve it with cold cooked asparagus or broccoli, sprinkled with soy sauce and sesame seeds, and warm biscuits or rolls and you have a complete hot-weather supper.

CHICKEN QUESADILLAS

eight 8-inch flour tortillas

2 cups chopped cooked barbecued or roast chicken (or barbecued pork)

½ cup minced scallion

4 teaspoons minced fresh jalapeño pepper (or canned chile peppers to taste)

4 teaspoons minced cilantro

2 cups grated Monterey Jack cheese

The one thing that Mother made for our lunches more often than anything else was some variation on a basic grilled cheese (read Velveeta) sandwich. Pat's favorite combination was GC and fried bologna, whereas Bonnie swore by GC and fried Spam. It shows just how far we've come when we realize that those early grilled cheese sandwiches have metamorphosed into our present lunchtime favorite south-of-the-border "sandwich": quesadillas. The Velveeta has been replaced with Monterey Jack cheese, chicken or pork has become the partnering ingredient of choice, and the breadiness has been reduced with thin crisp flour tortillas. This recipe is fast and easy to prepare and is just as tasty yet considerably healthier than those childhood grilled cheese sandwiches, especially if you use whole-wheat tortillas and low-fat cheese.

Sprinkle 1 tortilla with ½ cup of chicken, 2 tablespoons scallion, 1 teaspoon jalapeño pepper, 1 teaspoon cilantro, and ½ cup cheese, leaving a ½-inch border, and top it with a second tortilla, pressing down lightly. Assemble 3 more quesadillas in the same manner. In a nonstick skillet at least 10 inches in diameter and lightly coated with cooking spray, cook one of the quesadillas over moderate heat until the underside is crisp and lightly browned and invert it onto a plate that has been lightly coated with cooking spray. Recoat the skillet with cooking spray, carefully slide the quesadilla back into the skillet, and cook it until the other side is crisp and lightly browned. Slide the quesadilla onto a serving plate, cut it into wedges, and serve it immediately. Cook the remaining quesadillas in the same manner. Now, if you are fortunate enough to own an electric panini press or sandwich grill, it will make even better quesadillas faster. Serves 8 to 10 as a snack or appetizer and 4 as a light entrée.

P&B's Hints: For a vegetarian version, replace the meat with rinsed and well drained black or pinto beans. Use any kind of cheese that strikes your fancy. For variety try adding sun-dried tomatoes, chopped avocado, chopped cooked chorizo or other sausage, various kinds of peppers, and a spoonful of sour cream on top. Use smaller tortillas to create hors-d'oeuvre wedges.

TURKEY PICCATA

Grandma made fried chicken and Mother made fried chicken, and the main difference between the two versions was FAT: Grandma's was deep-fried, Mother's was pan-sautéed. There was no arguing that Grandma's tasted best, but even she had to admit that maybe all that deliciously fat-laden crispiness wasn't exactly good for you. Deep-fried chicken has for the most part been replaced in our diets with quicker-cooking, lighter poultry alternatives. One of our favorite options is this Italianate piccata-style turkey breast with a refreshingly piquant, quick-and-easy sauce. The dish can also be made with chicken cutlets, pounded thin between sheets of wax paper, and is great too with veal if you can get good tender veal cutlets.

In a nonreactive saucepan combine the stock, wine, and garlic and cook the mixture over high heat, stirring occasionally, until it is reduced to 1 cup. Reduce the heat to moderate, whisk in the flour mixture, and cook the sauce, stirring often, until it is thickened slightly. Swirl in the butter followed by the lemon juice, capers, and salt and remove the pan from the heat. Sprinkle the cutlets with salt and pepper and dust them with flour. In a large skillet sauté the cutlets in 1 tablespoon of the oil, adding more as necessary, over moderately high heat for a minute or two on each side, or until they are lightly browned and springy to the touch, then transfer them to a platter. Reduce the heat to moderately low, add the sauce to the skillet, stirring in any pan juices from the sautéing, and heat the sauce until it is hot. Pour the sauce over the cutlets and sprinkle the dish with the parsley. Serves 2 to 4.

1¼ cups chicken stock or broth

⅓ cup dry white wine

1 large garlic clove, minced

1 tablespoon flour, dissolved in 2 tablespoons chicken broth or water

1 tablespoon butter

1 tablespoon lemon juice, or to taste

1 tablespoon drained small capers

½ teaspoon salt

1 pound thin-sliced turkey cutlets

flour for dusting

1 to 2 tablespoons mild olive oil

1 to 2 tablespoons minced parsley

TURKEY AND MUSHROOM PATTIES

½ pound mushrooms (half thinly sliced, half finely chopped)

1¼ pounds ground turkey or chicken

2 cups bread crumbs made from stale white bread

1 egg, lightly beaten

½ cup minced onion

1 small garlic clove, minced

2 teaspoons Worcestershire sauce

1 teaspoon dried thyme

1 teaspoon salt

several grinds of pepper

3 tablespoons butter

2 tablespoons flour, plus extra for dusting

1 cup whole milk

1 tablespoon dry Sherry or vermouth (optional)

Grandma used her cumbersome hand-cranked meat grinder to double-grind the ingredients for her chicken patties, one reason that the finished product was so light in texture, smooth and silky. We actually prefer a little more texture, and with the ground turkey or chicken now readily available in the supermarket we can create turkey patties in no time flat. Grandma's version involved crisp-frying in gobs of butter. Our slightly healthier adaptation is sautéed using much less butter, resulting in a softer exterior, which we bathe in a light sauce. The simplicity and homey flavors of these patties make them a comfort-food favorite with kids and grownups alike.

In a large bowl combine the chopped mushrooms (reserve the sliced ones), turkey, bread crumbs, egg, onion, garlic, 1 teaspoon of the Worcestershire sauce, ½ teaspoon of the thyme, salt, and pepper (we find using your hands works best). Shape the mixture into 2½- to 3-inch patties, ½ to ¾ inch thick, and dust them with flour. In a large skillet cook the patties in the butter in batches over moderate heat for 6 to 7 minutes per side, or until they are lightly browned and cooked through. Keep the patties warm in a serving dish. Add the sliced mushrooms to the skillet and cook them over moderately low heat, stirring often, for 2 to 3 minutes, or until they are softened. Sprinkle the mushrooms with the 2 tablespoons flour and the remaining ½ teaspoon thyme and cook the mixture, stirring, for 1 minute. Stir in the milk and cook the mixture, stirring, for 2 to 3 minutes, or until it is thickened. Stir in the Sherry, the remaining teaspoon Worcestershire sauce, and salt and pepper to taste. Serve the patties topped with the sauce. Serves 4.

P&B's Hints: The patties and sauce can be made ahead and kept separate, covered and chilled, for later reheating in the microwave. The patties and sauce also freeze well either together or separately.

TURKEY MEAT LOAF

Because meat loaf was an inexpensive dish that could be stretched over several meals and used for lunch box sandwiches, we saw a lot of it in our growing-up years. Although Grandma and Mother both made it with a home-ground combination of beef, pork, and veal, we gradually grew to prefer this lighter turkey version. The heavy hand-cranked meat grinder that Grandma and Mother used sits idle these days. Considering the ready availability of packaged ground meat and poultry today, the following recipe seems wimpishly easy to prepare.

Preheat the oven to 375° F. In a skillet cook the onion and garlic in the butter over moderately low heat until they are softened. Stir in the bread crumbs, transfer the mixture to a large bowl, and let it cool slightly. In a small bowl beat the eggs with the milk and Worcestershire sauce and add the mixture to the bowl. Add the turkey, crumbled, the parsley, thyme, and salt and combine the mixture well (we find using your hands works best). Transfer the mixture to a 9- by 5-inch loaf pan, lightly coated with cooking spray, spread the top with the ketchup, and bake the loaf for 1 hour, or until a meat thermometer inserted in the center of the loaf registers 170° F. Let the meat loaf rest in the pan for 5 minutes before slicing. Serves 6 to 8.

1½ cups finely chopped onion

2 garlic cloves, crushed and minced

1 tablespoon butter or vegetable oil

1¼ cups fresh bread crumbs

2 eggs

¼ cup milk

½ teaspoon Worcestershire sauce

2 pounds ground turkey

2 tablespoons minced parsley

½ teaspoon dried thyme

1 teaspoon salt

2 tablespoons ketchup

P&B's Hints: This is an extremely versatile basic recipe. It can be embellished by adding to the onion mixture in the skillet ½ cup of any of the following ingredients: finely shredded fresh spinach, finely diced red or green pepper, finely chopped mushrooms or zucchini, and minced carrot or celery. Substitute dried sage for the thyme or use 1½ teaspoons fresh herbs in place of the dried. Or give the dish an Asian flavor by using the vegetable oil instead of butter, adding ½ teaspoon Asian sesame oil, substituting 2 tablespoons soy sauce for the Worcestershire sauce, omitting the thyme, and replacing the parsley with minced fresh cilantro. For an Italianate version eliminate the Worcestershire sauce and thyme and add 2 tablespoons grated Parmesan and 1 teaspoon each of red pepper flakes, dried basil, and dried oregano.

SEAFOOD

Seafood in general was not Grandma's preferred choice of a main course. She cooked and ate it mainly because Grandpa liked to fish, plus seafood was, in those days, a thrifty alternative to meat and poultry. Growing up, we could expect to find something fishy on the supper table almost every weekend. If Grandpa wasn't going out angling on Saturday, Mother served fish on Friday, bought from the local market. Many people observed a meatless Friday custom back then, so the fish supply was usually plentiful and freshest that day. Grandma never lavished the care and attention on seafood that she did on other more favored ingredients. The memory of her soupy poached finnan haddie still haunts us. Mother, too, was never an enthusiastic fish cook, adopting a straightforward breaded-and-fried approach. We, however, are particularly fond of seafood and today it figures prominently in our diets, not only for health considerations, but because we have a broader selection of fresh fish and shellfish to choose from and a vast array of condiments with which to embellish them—any day of the week.

SHRIMP AND RICE NEWBURG

4½ cups chicken broth

1½ cups long-grain rice

1 tablespoon prepared basil pesto

1 shallot, minced

1 garlic clove, minced

3 tablespoons butter

4 tablespoons flour

1 cup milk

an 11-ounce can cream of shrimp soup

¾ cup sour cream

1 tablespoon dry vermouth or Sherry (optional)

2 pounds medium shelled and deveined cooked shrimp, halved

8 hard-boiled eggs, cut into ¾-inch pieces

½ cup shredded Monterey Jack cheese

¾ cup fresh bread crumbs or panko

Finnan haddie (smoked haddock) came in a tin, was packed with intense smoky flavor, was inexpensive, and seemed to be a permanent fixture on both Grandma's and Mother's pantry shelf. When Mother mixed it with chopped hard-boiled eggs and served it in a cream sauce over rice, it was a tolerable comfort food concoction. In that form it occasionally continues to find its way onto our tables, albeit not when our husbands have any input into the menu. Upscaling Mother's recipe with the substitution of shrimp plus a few savory additions, we have created a Newburg-style dish that has just enough sophistication to hold its own in front of company on the buffet table. The recipe can be halved successfully.

In a large saucepan bring the broth to a boil, stir in the rice and the pesto, and simmer the mixture, covered, for 20 minutes, or until the broth is absorbed and the rice is just tender. While the rice is cooking, in another saucepan cook the shallot and the garlic in the butter over moderately low heat, stirring, until the shallot is softened. Stir in the flour and cook the mixture, stirring, for 2 minutes. Whisk in the milk and then the soup and cook the mixture, stirring, for 5 minutes, or until it is thickened. Remove the pan from the heat and let the sauce cool slightly. Stir in the sour cream, vermouth, and salt and pepper to taste and in a large bowl combine the sauce with the cooked rice. Preheat the oven to 350° F. Gently fold the shrimp and eggs into the rice mixture, turn the Newburg into a 9- by 13-inch baking dish, lightly coated with cooking spray, and top it with the cheese and bread crumbs. Spray the top lightly with cooking spray and bake the casserole for 35 minutes, or until it is heated through. Put the casserole under the broiler briefly, if necessary, to brown the crumbs. Serves 8 to 10.

P&B's Hints: Full-fat, low-fat, or no-fat dairy products all work fine here. The dish can be made (minus the topping) up to 8 hours ahead and kept, covered and chilled. When ready to cook, add the cheese and crumb topping, and bake the dish as above for 45 minutes. Or you can reheat it without the cheese and crumbs in the microwave, stirring halfway through, until heated through (about 10 minutes), then sprinkle on the topping and put the dish under the broiler briefly to melt the cheese and brown the crumbs.

GARLIC PAPRIKA SHRIMP

Grandpa was the family angler, and when he went out deep-sea fishing with his buddies he usually brought home, along with the day's catch, a couple pounds of shrimp to be cooked as a prelude to the main fish course. With big bib-like napkins tucked in our collars, we ate messy platefuls of shrimp that had been simply boiled with some Old Bay seasoning, shelling them (skipping that fussy deveining step), and dipping them in cups of melted butter. Although we occasionally continue the tradition of a "shrimp boil," we now generally serve shrimp in this more dressed-up, Spanish-influenced manner. The shrimp can be shelled and deveined up to a day in advance, which then makes this a very quick dish to put together for entertaining— and your company won't get their nice clothes messed up eating it.

In a nonreactive skillet heat the olive oil, garlic, paprika, cumin, and salt over moderate heat, stirring, until the mixture begins to sizzle. Add the shrimp and cook them, tossing and stirring them to coat them well with the oil mixture, until they turn pink and are just cooked through. Add the cilantro and lemon juice and toss the mixture together well. Serve the shrimp in small bowls with warm bread for sopping up the sauce. Or serve the shrimp mixture in a shallow dish with toothpicks for spearing as an hors d'oeuvre. The shrimp can be served hot, warm, or room temperature. Serves 6 as a starter and 4 as an entrée.

4 tablespoons extra virgin olive oil

3 garlic cloves, minced

2 teaspoons mild Spanish paprika (preferably smoked)

¾ teaspoon ground cumin

1 teaspoon salt

1½ pounds large or extra-large shrimp, shelled and deveined

2 tablespoons minced cilantro

2 tablespoons lemon juice

crusty bread as an accompaniment

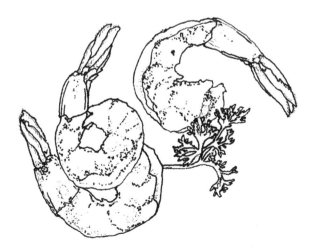

THAI-STYLE COCONUT CURRY SHRIMP

2 small zucchini, diced (about 1 cup)

1 small red bell pepper, seeded and diced (about 1 cup)

1 cup chopped onion

2 teaspoons vegetable oil

2 large garlic cloves, minced

4 teaspoons curry powder

1 teaspoon ground cumin

¼ teaspoon chili powder

¾ cup fat-free half-and-half or light cream

½ cup lite unsweetened coconut milk

½ teaspoon salt, or to taste

1 pound shelled and deveined medium shrimp (about 1¼ pounds unshelled)

2 teaspoons cornstarch

4 teaspoons fresh lime juice

3 to 4 tablespoons minced cilantro

steamed rice as an accompaniment

Shrimp has always ranked high among our favorite foods. As our dining experience broadened, however, we gradually strayed from the simplicity of drawn-butter dipping to more international preparations. This Thai-style dish is light and pretty easy to prepare—except for shelling and deveining the shrimp. So, if you are in a real hurry, splurge on the already prepared shrimp at your market seafood counter or (if really desperate) use a bag of frozen and defrosted shrimp. The dish is undeniably better made with fresh shrimp, but the sauce is so delicious that the degree of difference in taste and texture may be a worthwhile trade-off in time saving.

In a skillet cook the zucchini, red pepper, and onion in the oil over moderately low heat, stirring occasionally, until they are softened. Add the garlic, curry powder, cumin, and chili powder and cook the mixture, stirring, for 2 minutes. Stir in the half-and-half, coconut milk, and salt and cook the mixture, stirring, for 3 minutes, or until it is combined and simmering. Add the shrimp and cook the mixture, stirring it together lightly, for 5 minutes, or until the shrimp turn pink and are just cooked through. (If using already cooked shrimp cook the mixture until the shrimp are just heated through.) Stir in the cornstarch, dissolved in a small amount of water, the lime juice, and cilantro and cook the mixture, stirring , until the sauce is thickened slightly. Serve the curry with steamed rice. Serves 4.

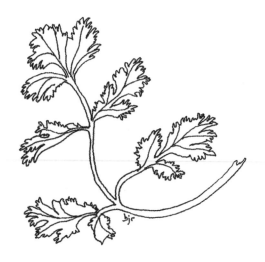

SEAFOOD POTATO CAKES

As grade-schoolers, we went through a stage when frozen fish sticks were our favorite thing—Grandma was appalled. Mother agreed they might not be all that wholesome, but they were guaranteed to please and were an easy out for her when time was short. We've come a long way from those fish sticks in the fish cakes that we make today. Sautéing has replaced deep frying, and the seafood has been partnered with mashed potato and any number of cooked vegetables, herbs, and spicings. As such, the cakes are a great way to use up leftovers and, with a side salad, they become a speedy light meal.

In a bowl combine well the mashed potatoes, crab meat, scallion, Old Bay seasoning, and salt and with lightly oiled hands shape the mixture into 6 cakes about 1 inch thick. (The cakes can be made up to this point a day ahead and kept, covered and chilled.) Coat the cakes with the bread crumbs or panko, pressing lightly so that the coating adheres well. In a large skillet sauté the cakes in 2 teaspoons oil over moderately high heat, adding more oil as necessary, until they are golden brown on both sides and heated through. Makes 6 cakes.

2 cups leftover mashed potatoes (or packaged if you don't happen to have leftover)

1 pound crab meat, excess moisture squeezed out (or other chopped cooked seafood)

⅓ cup minced scallion tops

1 teaspoon Old Bay seasoning, or to taste

½ teaspoon salt, or to taste

bread crumbs or panko for coating the seafood cakes

olive oil or butter for sautéing

P&B's Hints: We have given the basic bare bones recipe here, which can be augmented with a variety of vegetables, herbs, and spices. Cooked asparagus, broccoli, spinach, and celery have all found their way into the mix, as have parsley, chives, cilantro, dill, and tarragon. We have even gone so far as to add soy sauce, sesame oil, and the crunch of minced water chestnuts for an Asian touch. If money is no object, fresh lump crab meat is our top pick for the seafood element, but smoked salmon, shrimp, salt cod, canned tuna, and a whole gamut of leftover cooked fish have made successful appearances as well.

FLOUNDER AND FENNEL GRATIN

1½ pounds skinned fillets of flounder, sole, sea trout, or other mild white fish

1 cup finely chopped fennel bulb or celery if you prefer a milder taste

¾ cup finely chopped onion

2 tablespoons olive oil

1 garlic clove, minced

½ teaspoon dried herbes de Provence or crumbled dried thyme

¾ teaspoon salt

a few grinds of pepper

2½ cups coarse bread crumbs

3 tablespoons grated Parmesan, or to taste

Although we love fish, not all of our family and friends share our culinary sentiments. Both Grandma and Mother regularly served flounder and other mild white fish, generally coated with the usual sequential mixture of flour, egg, and crumbs and then deep-fried or pan-sautéed in lots of butter. The fish was certainly tasty, but not particularly exciting and more fat-laden than we prefer these days, plus the stale aroma of fried fish tended to linger in the air for days afterward. In this variation, the light bread-crumb crispness that we like is retained, fennel adds a subtle provençal accent, and the oven-baking eliminates any frying messiness or smell. Also, the hint of Thanksgiving stuffing conveyed in the topping is a flavor ploy guaranteed to win over the most dedicated carnivore.

Preheat the oven to 350° F. In a 9- by 12-inch baking dish, lightly coated with cooking spray, arrange the flounder fillets, skinned side down, in one layer. In a skillet sauté the fennel and the onion in the oil over moderately low heat until they are softened slightly, add the garlic, herbs, salt, and pepper, and cook the mixture, stirring, until the vegetables are softened. In a bowl combine the fennel mixture with the bread crumbs, tossing the mixture together lightly until it is well combined. Arrange the crumb mixture on the fish, sprinkle it with the Parmesan, and bake the mixture in the upper third of the oven for 20 minutes, or until the fish flakes when tested with a fork and the crumb mixture is nicely browned and crisp. If a crisper topping is desired, put the dish under the broiler for several minutes. Serves 4.

P&B's Hints: This bread crumb mixture is equally good as a topping over boneless, skinless chicken breasts or turkey cutlets.

QUICK ASIAN-FUSION FISH

When living in a small apartment with windows that didn't open, we soon learned that frying fish the way Grandma did was a sure way to get the entire floor of neighbors annoyed at you. To cut down on the odor of deep frying as well as its trans fat quotient, we opted for stovetop poaching with a light, healthy broth that blends East-West flavors and cooking techniques. Although we usually make this dish with filleted fish, it is also great with shelled and deveined shrimp.

Holding the knife at a 45-degree angle, cut the fish crosswise into about 2-inch pieces. In a nonstick skillet at least 12 inches in diameter heat the ginger, scallion, and garlic in the sesame and canola oils over low heat until they are warmed through and aromatic. Stir in the orange juice, soy sauce, rice wine, and hoisin sauce and nestle the fish into the sauce in one layer as much as possible. Simmer the mixture, covered, over moderate heat, shaking the pan occasionally to distribute the liquid over the fish and to prevent sticking, for 3 to 5 minutes, or until the fish just flakes when tested with a fork. Sprinkle the dish with the cilantro and serve it with steamed rice. Serves 2 to 4.

1 pound skinned fillets of flounder, cod, sea bass, or grouper

1 tablespoon peeled and minced gingerroot

2 tablespoons minced scallion, including the green tops

1 teaspoon minced garlic

1 teaspoon Asian sesame oil

1 teaspoon canola or other vegetable oil

2 tablespoons orange juice

2 tablespoons soy sauce

1 tablespoon rice wine or medium-dry Sherry

1 tablespoon hoisin sauce

2 tablespoons minced cilantro (or flat-leafed Italian parsley)

steamed rice as an accompaniment

SEAFOOD LINGUINE MARINARA

1 pound skinless firm white fish fillets such as cod, sea bass, or grouper

1 cup chopped onion

¾ cup diced green bell pepper

⅓ cup diced celery

1 large garlic clove, minced

1½ teaspoons minced fresh oregano or ½ teaspoon dried

1 tablespoon olive oil

a 14½-ounce can diced tomatoes with the juice or 2 cups peeled, seeded, and diced fresh tomato

3 tablespoons chopped pitted oil-cured black olives

¼ teaspoon salt

a large pinch of sugar

chopped parsley, chives, or cilantro for garnish

cooked linguine as an accompaniment

Tomatoes were the centerpiece of both our family's and Grandma's vegetable gardens, and in the summer months they cropped up regularly on the table in everything from salad to spaghetti sauce. Although Grandma partnered tomato with seafood—as in her version of clam chowder—serving the combo as a pasta topping would be, to her mind, bizarre at best. Except for some container patio plants, we no longer grow tomatoes, relying instead on farmers markets in summer and on canned goods in winter, which we find generally have better flavor and texture than the gas-ripened supermarket produce. Served with a green salad or a side of spinach or broccoli rabe, this Italianate dish makes a quick and easy light meal in summer or winter. If you prefer shrimp to fish fillets, it too works well in this dish.

Holding the knife at a 45-degree angle, cut the fish crosswise into about 1½-inch pieces. In a nonreactive, nonstick skillet at least 12 inches in diameter cook the onion, green pepper, celery, garlic, and oregano in the oil over moderately low heat, stirring occasionally, until the vegetables are softened. Add the tomato, olives, salt, and sugar, simmer the mixture, stirring occasionally, until it is heated through, then nestle the fish into the mixture in one layer as much as possible. Simmer the mixture, covered, shaking the pan occasionally to better distribute the vegetable mixture over the fish and prevent sticking, for 3 to 5 minutes, or until the fish just flakes when tested with a fork. Sprinkle the mixture with the chopped herbs and carefully spoon portions of it over cooked linguine. Serves 2 to 4.

SCALLOP SEVICHE

We have always loved the beach, and on summer weekends our family spent long days escaping the heat at a nearby seaside park. Toward sundown, with lips blue from the chilly salt water and skin pink from a full day's sun, everyone piled into the old Buick and headed off to our favorite down-home fish house. There we kids gorged ourselves on fried clams while the adults downed raw oysters, which to us were slimy and disgusting. Years later, through our travels and dining experiences in ethnic restaurants, we made the discovery that raw seafood could be "cooked" with citrus juices. We subsequently introduced a skeptical mother into the exotic world of seviche, and multiple variations on this deliciously refreshing, healthy preparation became a favorite of all.

Remove and discard the tough "foot" from the scallops and cut the scallops into ½-inch pieces. In a ceramic or glass bowl combine the lime and lemon juices, oil, garlic paste, and jalapeño pepper, add the scallops, and toss the mixture together well. Chill the mixture, covered, stirring occasionally, for 2 hours, or until the scallops have turned whiter and are no longer translucent. (The mixture can be chilled, covered, overnight.) Add the tomatoes, scallion, cilantro, and avocado and toss the mixture together lightly until all the ingredients are well coated with the citrus mixture. With a slotted spoon divide the seviche among lettuce-lined salad plates, or for a fancier presentation serve the seviche in large scallop shells (available at cookware stores). Serves 8 as a first course.

1½ pounds very fresh sea scallops

1 cup fresh lime juice

½ cup fresh lemon juice

¼ cup extra virgin olive oil

1 small garlic clove, minced and mashed to a paste with 1½ teaspoons salt

1 tablespoon minced jalapeño pepper (optional)

2 cups halved and seeded grape tomatoes

¼ cup minced scallion, including the green tops

¼ cup minced cilantro

½ cup diced avocado (dice and add the avocado just before serving to preserve texture and color)

lettuce as an accompaniment

SEAFOOD PASTA SALAD

4 cups mixed bite-size pieces of cooked seafood

½ pound small or medium pasta shells or cavatelli, cooked al dente, drained well, and cooled

1 cup thinly sliced celery

½ cup finely diced red bell pepper

¼ cup chopped scallion, including the green tops

2 tablespoons chopped dill (or other favorite herbs such as parsley or cilantro to taste)

¾ cup reduced-fat mayonnaise

⅓ cup low-fat sour cream

1 garlic clove, minced and mashed to a paste with ¼ teaspoon salt

4 teaspoons bottled horseradish

In Grandma's mind pasta (noodley sorts of things) and salad (mainly lettuce with tomato and dressing) were two separate entities, to be served as such. We, however, have wholeheartedly embraced the concept of combining the two, and some version of the following dish has become a summer staple in our houses. We are partial to it because it is extremely versatile and works well with any combination of shrimp, scallops, crab meat, flavored seafood sticks, squid rings and tentacles, or cubed cooked firm-fleshed fish such as salmon. It can be made up to a day ahead and still looks like a million bucks and tastes pretty good too. Serve small portions of it as a first course or larger portions atop a plate of salad greens with garden tomatoes as a lunch or light supper dish.

In a large bowl toss together the seafood, pasta, celery, red pepper, scallion, and herbs. In a small bowl whisk together the mayonnaise, sour cream, garlic, and horseradish. Gently fold the dressing into the seafood mixture until the two are well combined, add salt and pepper to taste, and chill the salad, covered, for at least 2 hours or overnight. Serves 6 to 8 as a main course and 8 to 10 as a first course.

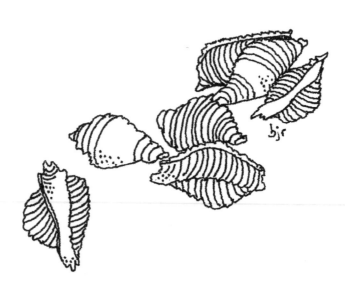

SALMON BURGERS

Grandma and Mother were firm believers in the health benefits of omega oils decades before they became the nutritionists' hot button. Because Grandpa loved to fish (it got him out of the house and out from under Grandma's thumb for the whole of Saturday), we often enjoyed fresh local varieties such as striped bass and bluefish whenever he was lucky with his catch. More exotic fish such as salmon came in a can as far as we knew. From this canned stock—especially tuna and salmon—Grandma and Mother made a tidal wave of fish cakes and loaves. None of these rated among our favorite things, but consuming them at least gave us a reprieve from the spoonfuls of cod liver oil to which we were regularly subjected. Today we are spoiled with an abundance of fresh and farmed seafood from around the world, and we only wish Grandma were still around so that we could whip up a batch of these fabulously light and savory salmon burgers for her. This recipe also makes great tuna burgers.

Finely chop the salmon (this works best done by hand as a food processor tends to mash it together). In a bowl combine well the egg, mustard, lemon juice, ricotta, cilantro, scallion, and garlic paste, add the bread crumbs and the salmon, and combine the mixture gently with your hands. Shape the mixture into 4 patties, transferring them to a plate that has been lightly coated with cooking spray, as they are shaped. The burgers may be chilled, covered, at this point for several hours (chilling the burgers will help them hold their shape). Spray the burgers lightly with cooking spray and in a nonstick skillet cook them over moderately high heat until they are lightly browned on both sides and just cooked through. Serve the burgers on buns with your favorite condiments. Makes 4 burgers.

1 pound skinless salmon fillet or fresh tuna

1 egg, lightly beaten

2 teaspoons Dijon-style mustard, or to taste

2 to 3 teaspoons lemon juice, or to taste

1 tablespoon ricotta cheese

2 tablespoons minced cilantro or parsley

2 scallions, minced

1 garlic clove, minced and mashed to a paste with ½ teaspoon salt

¾ cup fresh bread crumbs

burger buns

P&B's Hints: The burgers can also be prepared like crab cakes, coating them with additional bread crumbs or panko before spraying and cooking. (For appetizer-size portions shape into 6 patties). Make them Scandinavian-style by substituting dill for the cilantro and sour cream for the ricotta. Make them Asian-style by adding ¼ teaspoon Asian sesame oil and 1 teaspoon minced gingerroot and replacing the lemon juice with soy sauce and the ricotta with 2 teaspoons hoisin sauce.

ASIAN-STYLE GRILLED SALMON

6 salmon steaks, each ⅓ to ½ pound

½ cup soy sauce

⅓ cup honey

¼ cup ketchup

1 tablespoon hoisin sauce

2 garlic cloves, put through a garlic press or crushed and minced

minced cilantro for garnish

When we were growing up, a backyard barbecue fired with charcoal briquettes had become a summertime institution in suburban America. Grandma never fully warmed to the idea of grilling over fake rocks doused with flammable liquid, a practice she viewed as a less than civilized way to cook. Mother loved it because it took cooking heat out of the kitchen, and Daddy loved it as it was about as close as he was likely get his daughters to a campfire. We, too, love an outdoor barbecue (especially now that our grill is gas- rather than briquette-fired) and the simplicity and conviviality of picnic-style summer entertaining. This easy marinade/glaze is an Asian takeoff on the tomato and molasses basting sauce that Grandma favored for many of her oven-roasted dishes.

In a shallow dish arrange the salmon steaks in one layer. In a small bowl combine the soy sauce, honey, ketchup, hoisin sauce, and garlic, pour the mixture over the salmon, and turn the steaks so that they are well coated with the mixture. Let the salmon marinate in the mixture, covered and chilled, for at least 2 hours (overnight is okay). Grill the steaks over high heat, basting them and turning them until they are caramelized and just flake when tested near the bone with a fork. Serve the salmon sprinkled with the cilantro. Serves 6.

P&B's Hints: Although salmon steak is our first choice to go with this saucing, we have also used it successfully with thick salmon fillets, other firm-fleshed fish such as swordfish, and skewered shrimp and sea scallops.

SALMON GRATINÉE

As the fish that Grandpa caught on his angling excursions tended to arrive home whole rather than filleted, Grandma generally ended up oven-roasting his catch with lots of lemon and butter. Although there were skin and bones to contend with in the eating, they served to keep the fish moist, tender, and more flavorful in the cooking. We think one reason many people don't like fish is that it is frequently overcooked and dried out. For ease of preparation and eating, we now generally cook fillets rather than whole fish, but we've managed to seal in the moisture with a flavorful topping and by baking at a low temperature.

In a small bowl combine the bread crumbs, Parmesan, and nuts. In another small bowl combine the mayonnaise, herbs, lemon juice, and rind. Preheat the oven to 250° F. Lay the salmon, skin side down if the fillet is unskinned, on an ovenproof plate, lightly coated with cooking spray, and sprinkle it lightly with salt. Spread the mayonnaise mixture evenly over the fish and top it with the bread-crumb mixture. Bake the fish for 35 minutes, or until it just flakes when tested with a fork. Serves 4.

½ cup crisp buttered bread crumbs (recipe follows)

2 tablespoons grated Parmesan

2 tablespoons finely ground pecans or hazelnuts

2 tablespoons low-fat mayonnaise

1 tablespoon minced fresh herbs (whatever flavors you like best)

½ teaspoon lemon juice

½ teaspoon grated lemon rind

1½ pounds salmon fillet

BUTTERED BREAD CRUMBS

Grandma was big on buttered crumbs (well, she was big on buttered anything really), using them to top a variety of vegetable and casserole-style dishes. They added a nice textural contrast and a finishing touch to things like creamed cauliflower that might otherwise seem drab or uninteresting. We share her fondness for the topping to the point that we always have a jar of these crispy morsels on hand. This recipe is really just the proportional guideline that we use and the basic procedure. Vary the bread, depending on the flavor and texture that you desire.

In a small skillet melt the butter, add the bread crumbs, and toast them over low heat, stirring frequently, until they are evenly coated with the butter, lightly browned, and crisp. Transfer the crumbs to a small bowl, let them cool completely, and store them in an airtight container. Makes about 1 cup.

1 tablespoon salted butter

1 cup fresh bread crumbs (about 2 slices of sandwich-style bread)

TUNA NOODLES

Like most children, we loved "tuna noodles." It came in a can, was slippery, salty, and not too fishy tasting. Mother tolerated it as an extremely easy, inexpensive way to make us think we were getting a lunchtime treat. Grandma, however, delicately suggested that it was something better suited to feeding pigs than children and always insisted on making us tuna casserole from scratch—nice, but not the same as that wonderfully sinful, canned glop. Fortunately for the health of children everywhere, the company either stopped producing tuna noodles or they went out of business when we stopped eating it on a weekly basis. Eventually we opted for the homemade route, and over the years have adapted Grandma's original version, adding a variety of herbs, spices, and flavorings as well as peas, broccoli, asparagus, hard-boiled eggs, and even artichoke hearts. We have on occasion been known to use either cream of mushroom or celery soup instead of Grandma's white sauce; the microwave has become the reheating method of choice; and the golden topping is often crushed cornflakes, potato chips, or nachos. One thing, however, remains constant: Some form of tuna noodles ranks in our top ten most satisfying comfort foods.

TUNA NOODLE CASSEROLE WITH ASPARAGUS

This, our most current interpretation of "tuna noodles," has a down-home comfort that is guaranteed to please everyone from toddlers to the adultest of adults. It's sit-in-front-of-the-TV supper fare, yet presentable enough for a potluck dinner or Sunday brunch. It can be made ahead and refrigerated for later reheating. (We did try freezing it once and can say with relative assurance that you don't want to do that.) We love the flavor of tarragon in this dish, but, if it isn't your favorite taste, feel free to substitute oregano, thyme, dill, or another herb you prefer. For ease and speed in preparation we call for canned mushrooms as well as canned tuna, but you can go for greater sophistication and elegance by using equal amounts of cooked sliced fresh mushrooms and cooked and diced fresh tuna.

Cook the pasta according to the package directions until it is al dente, drain it, and reserve it. Blanch or steam the asparagus until it is crisp-tender and reserve it. In a bowl whisk together the milk, soup, mustard, Worcestershire sauce, and tarragon. In a 4-quart saucepan cook the celery, onion, and garlic in the butter over moderately low heat, stirring occasionally, until they are softened, add the flour, and cook the mixture, stirring, for 2 minutes. Stir the milk mixture into the celery mixture and cook the mixture, stirring occasionally, for 3 minutes, or until it is thickened and smooth. Fold in the cheese, mushrooms, tuna, eggs, pasta, and asparagus and cook the mixture, stirring gently, until it is heated through but not boiling. The tuna noodles can be served at once, sprinkled with crumbled potato chips. For a bit more elegance, however, transfer the mixture to a 2-quart baking dish, lightly coated with cooking spray, top it with buttered crumbs, and put it under the broiler for 2 minutes, or until the crumbs are crisp and browned. Tuna noodles can be made up to a day in advance and kept, covered and chilled, but do not add the crumbs until after the dish has been reheated (7 to 8 minutes in the microwave usually does it), then finish under the broiler. Serves 6.

½ pound your favorite pasta (we usually use linguine, broken into manageable lengths)

1½ cups asparagus, cut into 1-inch pieces

1¼ cups milk

an 11-ounce can cream of celery soup

2 teaspoons Dijon-style mustard or 1 teaspoon mustard powder

2 teaspoons Worcestershire sauce, or to taste

2 tablespoons chopped fresh tarragon or 2 teaspoons dried

2 celery stalks, thinly sliced

1 cup chopped onion

1 garlic clove, minced

3 tablespoons butter

2 tablespoons flour

1 cup shredded Swiss cheese

a 4-ounce can sliced mushrooms, drained

two 6-ounce cans water-packed tuna, well drained and crumbled

2 hard-boiled eggs, cut into ½-inch pieces

1 cup fresh bread crumbs, tossed with 2 tablespoons melted butter and ½ teaspoon garlic salt, or 1 cup crumbled potato chips

VEGGIES

During the summer months most of the vegetables we consumed came from either the garden or a variety of local farm stands, often merely makeshift roadside tables set out with whatever excess produce the household garden had yielded that week. During the height of the growing season we ate just-picked vegetables, which Grandma and Mother cooked simply in butter and adorned with nothing more than salt and pepper. Their wonderful fresh flavor enticed us into devouring quantities that would set new RDA records. Happily, today, farmers markets are seeing a revival even in urban centers, and a movement toward heirloom varieties and organic cultivation is producing veggies that prove the rich fresh flavors we remember from our childhood are not just wishful nostalgia.

MAPLE-GLAZED CARROTS

1½ pounds carrots, peeled, trimmed, and cut into sticks about 1½ inches long and ¼ to ½ inch thick

⅓ cup chopped scallion, white and green parts

2 tablespoons olive oil or butter

1 tablespoon fresh lime juice

1 teaspoon grated lime rind

¼ cup maple syrup

a few gratings of nutmeg

1 tablespoon minced cilantro or parsley

Carrots were right up there with spinach atop the list of what was "good for us" (a long list of less tasty things we had to get through to reach the dessert portion of the meal). Whereas spinach had Popeye helping to promote its consumption, carrots had no such champion. Raw carrot sticks were fine for snacking, but plain cooked carrots were, well, pretty blah. Grandma's boiled carrots were rated okay, but that was due more to all the butter and salt she added. Mother cut back on the butter for our father's cholesterol and added a bit of honey and cooked-down orange juice to liven up her boiled carrots. Today we have elevated the status of carrots another notch with a maple-glazing that draws on our New England roots and a touch of lime to balance the sweetness. Though veggies may never rival things like chocolate cake in popularity, these carrots are as good-tasting as they are good for you. They are also a handy choice for a company meal as they can be made ahead and served hot, at room temperature, or chilled.

In a steamer basket set over boiling water cook the carrots for 3 minutes, or until they are barely tender, and remove the steamer from the heat. In a skillet large enough to hold the carrots cook the scallion in the oil over moderate heat until it is softened slightly, add the carrots, lime juice, rind, maple syrup, and nutmeg, and cook the mixture until the carrots are tender and the liquid is reduced to a syrupy consistency. Add the cilantro and salt and pepper to taste. Serve the carrots hot, at room temperature, or chilled. Serves 6.

INDIAN-ACCENTED SPINACH

Spinach is good for you, right? Well, we certainly had that drilled into our heads, and the green stuff appeared with predictable regularity on the dinner table. Grandma's version rated best because it was never all that spinach-y as there was so much butter and cream in it. Mother cooked a lot of frozen spinach (the fresh often took too much time to wash and trim). Nowadays, with pre-washed baby spinach available in many grocery stores, we have returned to fresh and to Grandma's creamy approach, though with a lighter hand. Plus we've added some mild Indian spicing and relieved the intense greenness with chopped red pepper.

In a ceramic or glass casserole cook the spinach, covered, in batches if necessary, in the microwave for 3 minutes. Let the spinach cool, squeeze handfuls of it to remove the excess moisture, and chop it coarsely. In a large skillet cook the onion, garlic, red pepper, garam masala, and cumin in the butter over moderately low heat, stirring occasionally, until the vegetables are softened. Stir the cornstarch mixture to recombine it, add it to the skillet, and cook the mixture, stirring, until it is thickened slightly. Add the spinach and lemon rind and cook the mixture, tossing it together gently, until the spinach is well coated and heated through. Add the salt and pepper to taste. Serves 4 to 6.

24 ounces fresh baby spinach

1 cup minced onion

1 large garlic clove, crushed and minced

½ cup finely chopped red bell pepper

1 teaspoon garam masala

½ teaspoon ground cumin

1 tablespoon butter or extra virgin olive oil

2 teaspoons cornstarch dissolved in ½ cup fat-free half-and-half

½ teaspoon grated lemon rind

½ teaspoon salt, or to taste

SAUTÉED GREEN BEANS WITH PINE NUTS

1 pound slender young green beans (preferably haricots verts), trimmed and cut into 1- to 2-inch lengths

¾ cup minced red bell pepper (yellow or orange peppers or a mixture is also nice)

2 shallots, minced

1 large garlic clove, minced

1½ tablespoons extra virgin olive oil or butter

1 teaspoon salt

⅓ cup pine nuts, lightly toasted

Standing sentinel at the rear of Grandma's garden was a row of teepee-shaped trellises, their wood frames almost obscured by a camouflage of leafy pole bean vines. Pole beans were our preferred choice of "string beans" over the squat bush bean variety. Although we considered them okay as a side dish, they rose to star status when appearing in Grandma's sour cream-laced bean soup. Today we enjoy green beans on a regular basis, due in large part to the development of "stringless" varieties, plus the increased supermarket availability of the tender young French green beans known as haricots verts. The combination of red and green has made this dish a fixture at Christmas dinner, and its prepare-ahead, last-minute reheatability makes it a dinner party favorite.

In a saucepan of boiling salted water cook the beans until they are barely tender. Drain the beans in a colander, immerse them immediately in ice water to halt the cooking and preserve the green color, and when they are cool drain them well. In a large skillet cook the red pepper, shallots, and garlic in the oil over moderate heat until they are softened and remove the pan from the heat. When you are ready to serve the dish combine the green beans with the pepper mixture and heat the mixture, tossing it together lightly, until it is hot. (This can be done in the skillet on the stove over moderate heat or in a serving dish in the microwave.) Add the salt and pepper to taste and toss the beans with the pine nuts. Serves 6.

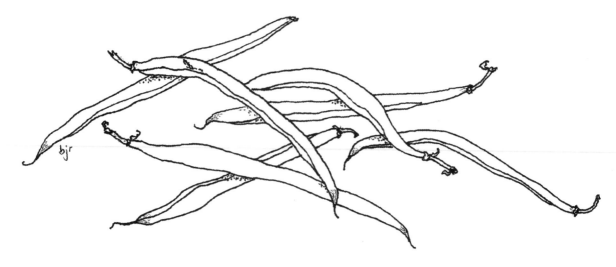

RATATOUILLE (PROVENÇAL MIXED VEGETABLES)

At the height of summer, when the garden was producing with something akin to adrenaline rush, we had more produce than our small family could consume. Grandma canned or pickled everything in sight. Although Mother quickly abandoned the tedium of canning, we still had nonstop vegetable combinations, based mainly on what was currently taking over the garden. As our acquaintance with French cooking expanded, we recognized that some of those combinations were really American cousins to the French dish ratatouille. These days, when local farm stands are overflowing with the basic components of that provençal classic—squash, peppers, eggplant, and tomatoes—we whip up a version of ratatouille, giving our childhood summer memories a Gallic accent. The proportions given here are more of a guideline than a set formula. We alter the dish almost every time we make it, readily adapting it to available produce and whims of taste. This recipe serves a crowd, but, even if you want a smaller amount for any given occasion, don't cut back. The minimal extra time invested to make this much pays off handsomely as the dish is even better reheated and it freezes beautifully, bringing a wonderful summery lift to a wintertime meal.

1 medium eggplant, cut into ¾-inch pieces (about 3 cups)

about 2 cups diced onion

4 large garlic cloves, minced

1 tablespoon olive oil

3 tablespoons tomato paste

1½ teaspoons dried herbes de Provence, oregano, or thyme

about 4 cups seeded and diced tomato

about 2 cups yellow squash, cut into ¾-inch pieces

about 2 cups zucchini, cut into ¾-inch pieces

about 2 cups red bell pepper, cut into ¾-inch pieces

1 small fennel bulb, coarsely chopped (optional)

3 cups chicken broth

½ cup white wine

a large pinch of sugar

1 teaspoon salt

¼ cup shredded basil

In a colander toss the eggplant with a sprinkling of salt, let it drain for 15 minutes, and pat it dry firmly with paper towels. In a large non-reactive Dutch oven or very large saucepan cook the onion and the garlic in the oil over moderately low heat, stirring occasionally, until they are softened slightly. Stir in the tomato paste and herbes de Provence, add the tomato, squashes, red pepper, fennel, and eggplant, and cook the mixture, stirring occasionally, until the vegetables are softened slightly. Add 2 cups of the broth, the wine, sugar, salt, and several grinds of pepper and cook the mixture at a bubbling simmer, stirring occasionally and adding more of the broth or water if the mixture becomes too dry, for 30 minutes, or until all the vegetables are soft and become a well-blended mixture. (You want a semi-stiff nonsoupy texture.) Add the basil and additional salt and pepper to taste. The ratatouille keeps, covered and chilled, for several days and can be served hot or cold. It also freezes well. Serves 14 to 16.

INDIAN-SPICED CAULIFLOWER

1 large cauliflower, cut into about 1-inch flowerets

1 pound potatoes (preferably Yukon Gold), peeled and cut into ½-inch cubes

5 tablespoons olive oil

2 teaspoons ground cumin

¼ teaspoon chipotle chile powder

¾ teaspoon salt, or to taste

1 cup diced onion

¼ cup diced red bell pepper

1 tablespoon seeded and minced jalapeño pepper

2 large garlic cloves, minced

1 tablespoon peeled and minced gingerroot

1 teaspoon garam masala

a few grates of nutmeg

¾ cup chicken broth

2 tablespoons minced cilantro

Grandma loved cauliflower and lavished the sort of attention on it that others might have considered an attempt—as the old saying goes—to make a silken purse out of a sow's ear. The way she prepared it most often was simply steamed, swimming in melted butter, and topped with toasted bread crumbs. Then there was creamed cauliflower, a Thanksgiving dinner staple, topped with bread crumbs and melted cheese. Some form of her culinary DNA must have been passed down to us because we too love the vegetable. We frequently make it just as Grandma did but have also added to her repertoire this favorite preparation of our own. Garam masala is an Indian spice mixture now available in most large supermarkets—don't leave it out, it really makes the dish.

Preheat the oven to 450° F. In a large lasagna-style baking dish or baking pan toss the cauliflower and the potatoes with 3 tablespoons of the oil, 1 teaspoon of the cumin, the chile powder, and ¼ teaspoon of the salt and roast the mixture, occasionally tossing it together gently, for 20 minutes, or until the cauliflower and potatoes are just tender. While the cauliflower mixture is roasting, in a skillet cook the onion, red pepper, jalapeño pepper, garlic, and ginger in the remaining 2 tablespoons oil with the garam masala, the remaining 1 teaspoon cumin, the remaining ½ teaspoon salt, and the nutmeg over moderately low heat, stirring occasionally, for 5 minutes, or until the onion is soft. Stir in the broth and simmer the mixture for 1 minute. Pour the contents of the skillet over the cauliflower mixture, toss the mixture together lightly until it is well combined, and roast it, covered with foil, for 5 minutes. Sprinkle the dish with the cilantro, toss it together lightly, and serve the cauliflower either hot or at room temperature. Serves 6.

P&B's Hints: Doing the cooking in a casserole-style dish makes for easy direct oven-to-table or buffet serving. If you have ghee (Indian-style clarified butter) and want to be more authentically Indian, substitute it for the olive oil.

HONEY-ROASTED ACORN SQUASH

The world was bigger in Grandma's day, and produce markets tended to be more local than global. Thus, the fresh vegetables that we ate were consumed on a more seasonal basis. Fall and winter meant acorn squash, which made its appearance on the table as little green-hulled boats, oven-roasted and brimming to the gunwales with a mixture of butter and brown sugar. It was one of our favorite vegetables, though admittedly, it was the caramel-like topping that appealed to us more than the flavor of the squash itself. Acorn squash remains one of our cold-weather staples, and, though we still favor a slightly sweet-tooth approach, we have tempered it with a touch of spice. Cutting up the squash makes for a prettier presentation, a slightly faster cooking time, and easier reheating in a microwave. This preparation also works well with butternut squash.

Preheat the oven to 375° F. Halve the squash lengthwise, scrape out and discard the seeds and stringy matter, and cut the halves crosswise into half moons at roughly 1-inch intervals (for smaller wedges, quarter the squash lengthwise before cross-cutting). In a large bowl combine the butter, maple syrup, honey, adobo sauce, cinnamon, nutmeg, and salt, add the squash, and turn the slices over in the sauce until they are well coated. Transfer the mixture to a 9- by 13-inch baking pan lined with foil, lightly coated with cooking spray, and arrange the squash slices in one layer. Bake the squash slices, turning them once halfway through the cooking, for 30 minutes, or until they are nicely caramelized and soft when tested with a fork. Serves 2 to 4.

1 acorn squash (about 1½ pounds), washed well, wiped dry, and the ends trimmed off

2 tablespoons butter, melted

¼ cup maple syrup

1 tablespoon honey

½ teaspoon sauce from canned chiles in adobo (optional but worth the trouble to find)

¼ teaspoon cinnamon

a pinch of nutmeg

a pinch of salt

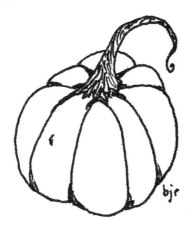

VEGETABLE PÂTÉ

1¼ cups puréed cooked broccoli (about ½ pound fresh)

1¼ cups puréed cooked cauliflower (about ½ head fresh)

1¼ cups puréed cooked carrots (about ½ pound fresh)

2 tablespoons minced cilantro

¼ teaspoon nutmeg

2 tablespoons minced white part of scallion

¼ teaspoon curry powder

¼ teaspoon ground cumin

4 eggs

⅓ cup half-and-half

3 tablespoons butter, melted

1 teaspoon salt

6 tablespoons flour

Generations of parents have spent countless hours looking for ways to get children to eat their vegetables. Facing an army of more sugar-laced and unctuously fat-laden foods, vegetables have the deck stacked against them in the flavor wars. Grandma and Mother launched the vegetable crusade early. In an era that predated mass-marketed baby food, they fed us mashed home-cooked vegetables, stirring in butter and cream to make them more appealing. And, although we went through a period of shunning many vegetables, we have come round to truly savoring them. This colorful pâté, enlivened with international spicing, is a grown-up version of those early baby foods. It is a great way to use up leftover cooked vegetables, but we like it enough to steam vegetables especially for it. Broccoli, cauliflower, and carrots is our favorite combination, but the basic formula works well with a number of other veggies as well—choose your favorites and season them with whatever herbs or spices you like. You may be surprised to find even veg-averse kids cleaning their plates. The pâté makes a light and elegant first course for a dinner party or a colorful addition to a buffet.

Preheat the oven to 350° F. Put the puréed broccoli, cauliflower, and carrots in 3 separate bowls and drain off any excess liquid. Stir the cilantro and nutmeg into the broccoli, the scallion and curry powder into the cauliflower, and the cumin into the carrot. In a blender or food processor blend together the eggs, half-and-half, butter, and salt. Add the flour, a tablespoon at a time, blending the mixture until the flour is completely incorporated and the mixture is smooth. Stir one third of the egg mixture into each of the 3 bowls, incorporating it well. Coat a loaf pan (about 9 by 5 inches) lightly with cooking spray, line it with wax paper, and lightly spray the paper. Spread the carrot mixture in the bottom of the pan, top it with the cauliflower mixture, and top that with the broccoli mixture. Cover the top with wax paper, and bake the pâté, set in a pan of hot water reaching halfway up the sides of the loaf pan, for 55 minutes, or until it is firm to the touch and pulls away slightly from the sides of the loaf pan. Let the pâté cool in the loaf pan on a rack for at least 10 minutes before removing the wax paper and slicing. Serve the pâté warm, at room temperature, or cold. The pâté keeps, covered with plastic wrap and chilled, for several days. Serves 8 to 10 as a side dish or first course.

CONFETTI SUMMER VEGETABLES

Make this quick and easy dish when you a have a supply of the freshest summer vegetables. It is simplicity itself, is virtually limitless in adaptability and versatility, and at the same time is fancy-looking enough for company occasions. Grandma's version—a succotash of sorts—always included lima beans or butter beans, which are hard to come by fresh in many places these days. The only reason you won't find limas in this recipe however is that they are one thing that both husbands adamantly refuse to eat.

In a large skillet cook the zucchini, onion, red pepper, and garlic in the oil over moderate heat, stirring occasionally, until the vegetables are softened, add the corn kernels, and cook the mixture, stirring occasionally, until the corn is just cooked through (you want it to retain a nice crisp crunch). Add the salt and pepper and sprinkle the vegetables with the desired individual herb or combination to taste. Serves 4 to 6.

2 medium zucchini, scrubbed, trimmed, and diced (about 2 cups)

1 good-sized onion, diced (about 1 cup)

1 medium red bell pepper, seeded and diced (about 1 cup)

1 large garlic clove, minced

1 tablespoon extra virgin olive oil or butter

2 or 3 ears of corn, shucked and the kernels cut from the cob (about 1 cup)

½ teaspoon salt, or to taste

freshly ground pepper to taste

minced fresh chives, oregano, scallion tops, basil, thyme, or cilantro to taste for garnish

GARLIC MASHED POTATOES

3 pounds russet, Idaho, or Yukon Gold potatoes, peeled and quartered

1 teaspoon salt, or to taste

garlic paste (recipe adjacent page) to taste

fat-free half-and-half to taste

extra virgin olive oil or softened butter to taste

white pepper to taste

To Grandma, potatoes were just potatoes. The array of these tubers in the market today would have set her head spinning. Yukon Gold, russet, Red Bliss, fingerling, new, and Peruvian purple, along with "all purpose," are just the tip of the iceberg. The mind-boggling selection requires a certain level of potato I.Q. in order to differentiate which varieties fall into the high, medium, or low starch categories and are thus best for which kind of preparation. High starch potatoes generally make the fluffiest, best mashed potatoes. Our choice is russet or Idaho, although the slightly lower starch Yukon Gold has a nice buttery mellowness. Don't let this stop you, however, from using whatever you might have on hand. Grandma's mashed potatoes were rich with butter and cream. We think ours are almost as good…and better for you.

In a large saucepan combine the potatoes with cold water to cover and ½ teaspoon of the salt, bring the water to a boil over moderate heat, and cook the potatoes for 15 minutes, or until they are just tender when pierced with a fork. Drain the potatoes well, return them to the pan, and heat them briefly to dry them out slightly. Put the potatoes through a ricer into a bowl, and stir in the remaining ½ teaspoon salt, the garlic paste, half-and-half, olive oil, and pepper. Or add all the ingredients to the potatoes in the pan and mash them together with a wire masher. (We find an electric mixer or food processor tends to make unpleasantly gummy mashed potatoes.) Serves 6.

P&B's Hints: If the mashed potatoes are being served with a flavorful gravy, they are fine as is. But, if they are an un-gravied side dish, we tend to liven them up a bit more. Snipped chives, scallion tops, or minced parsley improve the appearance, buttermilk substituted for the half-and-half adds a nice tang, or the potatoes can be combined deliciously with cooked mashed rutabaga, parsnip, or celery root. Although we do not recommend this, if the occasion is really desperate, we have been known to stir a stash of our homemade garlic paste into store-bought mashed potatoes or—don't let this get around—even a pot of rehydrated potato flakes.

GARLIC PASTE

Concerning garlic, we've observed that diners break down into two camps with very little middle ground: Either you love it or you won't touch the stuff. We are members of a garlic-loving clan, with the caveat that we prefer ours cooked, not raw. One garlic clove, at the very least, works itself into an overwhelming number of main and side dishes that we prepare routinely. Grandma and Mother believed that garlic warded off all sorts of maladies (recent studies suggest there's some truth to that folk remedy), but we eat it because we like the warm, mellow flavor it adds, transforming Plain Jane mashed potatoes, a simple soup or stew, or a bland pasta sauce into a much more exciting dish. We always have a supply of this savory paste on hand in the refrigerator or freezer.

garlic cloves, peeled

chicken stock or broth

extra virgin olive oil or melted butter

In a saucepan combine as many garlic cloves as you have energy to peel with enough chicken broth to cover them by ½ inch. Bring the broth to a boil over moderately high heat, and simmer the mixture, covered, until the garlic is very soft. Transfer the garlic with a slotted spoon to a food processor, add a few drizzles of olive oil, and purée the mixture, adding a little of the broth if necessary, until it is a smooth paste. Store the paste in a glass jar in the refrigerator for up to a week. The paste can also be frozen. Save the garlic-flavored broth as well, stored in the same manner, for use in soups, stews, or sauces.

P&B's Hints: Many supermarkets sell already peeled garlic, which makes this recipe a snap to prepare. Trim and rinse well commercially peeled garlic before proceeding with the recipe. We spoon the paste into ice cube trays, freeze it, and store the frozen cubes, well wrapped. As a little of the concentrated paste goes a long way, the cubes are a convenient way of portioning out smaller amounts of paste. Ditto for the garlic-flavored broth.

CORN

For us, corn has always held a place of honor in the hierarchy of foods. Although canned vegetables were commonplace in our childhood years, with few exceptions they were bland, mushy, colorless, tinny-tasting, and in Grandma's opinion to be eaten only in times of desperation. (Frankly, they haven't improved much over the years.) Corn, however, really wasn't all that bad. It could even be eaten straight from the can without having to be disguised in stews or with sauces. It was one of a very small number of canned vegetables rated A-OK by every family member. Because the minuscule freezer compartment of Mother's refrigerator ruled out frozen vegetables, it goes without saying that we had canned corn a lot—in corn bread, corn muffins, corn pudding, corn fritters, scalloped corn, and succotash.

Every summer, however, we all eagerly awaited the opening of Fairty's Farm Market— originally just a wooden shack in front of the fields of apples trees, vegetables, and the best fresh corn for miles around. It wasn't today's sweet, delicate (read that as "wimpy") Butter and Sugar corn, but solid, crunchy ears of deep golden yellow. While Mother was catching up on the local news with Mrs. Fairty, we would scamper around behind the shack to pick out a dozen so-called short ears for our dinner. They were "short" because they had already been dinner for someone else: the corn worms that had nibbled away the tiny, tender kernels at the tip of each ear. Sold for half price, short ears made an economy out of a luxury, and with just a side dish of fried Spam (yes, Spam), hot buttered corn-on-the-cob was the absolute best August supper.

SOUFFLÉED CORN PUDDING

We've done little to change Grandma's basic recipe for this popular comfort food. Rarely however do we leave it as plain as she did, plus we lighten it up with some fat-free substitutions in the dairy department. Some of our favorite additions include 1 cup shredded Cheddar or jalapeño Jack cheese, 1 teaspoon chili powder, ½ cup finely chopped green or red pepper, or ⅓ cup minced scallions. Add ½ cup minced ham, 4 slices crisp-cooked crumbled bacon, or ⅓ cup minced pepperoni and serve the dish with a salad for a light lunch or supper.

Preheat the oven to 350° F. Coat a 2-quart baking dish lightly with cooking spray. In a large bowl beat the egg yolks and stir in the milk and corn. In a small bowl combine the flour, cornmeal, baking powder, sugar, and salt. In a medium bowl beat the egg whites until they hold stiff peaks. Stir the flour mixture into the milk mixture and gently fold in the egg whites. Pour the mixture into the baking dish and bake the pudding for 1 hour, or until it is puffed and a tester inserted in the center comes out clean. Serves 6 to 8.

4 eggs, yolks and whites separated

1 cup milk

two 15-ounce cans creamed corn (or 1 can of creamed and 1 of corn kernels, well drained)

½ cup flour

½ cup yellow cornmeal

1 teaspoon baking powder

1 tablespoon sugar

1 teaspoon salt

SUPER-EASY CORN PUDDING

If time is in extra short supply, you can still get a corn pudding fix with this very easy side dish. It won't be as light or elegant as the souffléed version, but it goes together in a flash. If you have regular milk or half-and-half on hand and prefer it to evaporated milk, use it instead. For a simple brunch dish, fold in cooked and crumbled breakfast sausage. Leftovers are delicious reheated the next morning and topped with maple syrup.

Preheat oven to 350° F. In a bowl beat together well the eggs, milk, sugar, salt, and paprika, gradually beat in the flour, and fold in the corn and stuffing. Pour the mixture into a 1½-quart baking dish, lightly coated with cooking spray, and bake it for 45 minutes, or until it is lightly browned, springy to the touch, and a tester inserted in the center comes out clean. Serves 6.

3 eggs

a 12-ounce can evaporated milk

1 tablespoon sugar

1 teaspoon salt

¼ teaspoon paprika

½ cup self-rising flour

a 15-ounce can corn kernels, well drained

1 cup cornbread stuffing

VEGGIE BURGERS

1½ cups grated carrot

1 cup minced scallion

1 cup finely shredded fresh spinach

¾ cup finely minced celery

½ cup very finely chopped pecans or walnuts

¾ cup minced mushrooms

⅓ cup minced red bell pepper

2 garlic cloves, minced and mashed to a paste with 1 teaspoon salt

2 tablespoons minced parsley, cilantro, thyme, or oregano

2 eggs

2 tablespoons soy sauce

2 teaspoons Asian sesame oil

about 3 cups matzo meal or crushed saltine or oyster crackers

olive oil or butter for sautéing

Thinking back, we can't recall anything resembling a vegetarian restaurant, juice bar, or so-called health food store in the community where we grew up. And it wasn't until our college days that we dabbled in vegetarianism, which was making its way from hippie-dom to mainstream at the time. All of those hamburgers we had happily devoured as children were now viewed to be, if not downright immoral, at least ethically objectionable. Mother watched with bemused restraint as we worked our way through a variety of tofu-, bean-, and grain-based veggie burgers ranging in texture from library paste to sawdust. Gradually our approach to vegetarian fare evolved from an ethical to a health perspective, and the veggie burgers we now make are more texturally appealing and flavorful. Even Mother eventually came round to enjoying this version and variations on it. Use this recipe as a jumping off point for developing your own favorite vegetarian combination.

In a large bowl combine the carrot, scallion, spinach, celery, nuts, mushrooms, red pepper, garlic paste, and herbs, tossing the mixture together lightly with a large fork or your hands (the way we do it). Add the eggs, lightly beaten with the soy sauce and sesame oil, combining the mixture gently. Incorporate 1 cup of the matzo meal, or enough so that the mixture holds together well enough to shape into firm but still moist patties. Shape the mixture into 8 patties (the patties can be covered and chilled at this point for several hours). Dust the veggie burgers with the remaining matzo meal and in a skillet sauté them in 2 teaspoons oil over moderately high heat, adding more oil if necessary, until they are lightly browned on both sides and cooked through. Serves 8.

PORTOBELLO PAPRIKA (MOCK VEAL PAPRIKA)

As a quick, thrifty, vegetarian alternative to Grandma's veal paprika, this recipe has chunky mushrooms standing in for the meat. Ready in less than one fourth the time of the veal version, it retains the ethnic flavor and hearty texture of the original. The thick meaty portobello mushrooms, which are commonly found in many markets today, make a particularly good choice for this dish, though it will be pretty tasty with the ordinary white mushrooms as well.

In a saucepan cook the mushrooms and shallots in the butter over moderately high heat, stirring occasionally, for 5 minutes, or until the mushrooms are softened. Stir in the garlic, paprika, sugar, and salt, add the stock, and cook the mixture, stirring occasionally, for 10 minutes, or until the sauce is reduced by half and thickened slightly. Remove the pan from the heat and stir in the sour cream. Serve the mushroom paprika with noodles. Serves 2 to 4.

1 pound portobello mushrooms, cut into 1-inch chunks (or white mushrooms, halved or quartered if large)

2 large shallots or 1 medium onion, thinly sliced

1 tablespoon butter or vegetable oil

1 garlic clove, minced

1 tablespoon mild Hungarian paprika

¼ teaspoon sugar

¼ teaspoon salt

⅓ cup beef, chicken, or vegetable stock or broth

⅓ cup sour cream

cooked noodles as an accompaniment

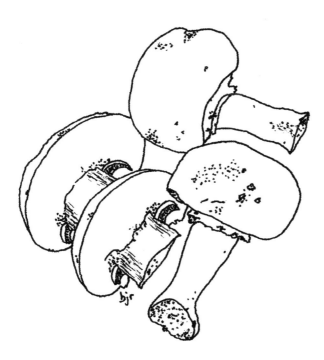

BASIC SAVORY BREAD PUDDING

3 cups bread cubes (made from any kind of stale bread, crusts discarded)

½ cup chopped cooked vegetables

½ cup chopped cooked ham, sausage, bacon, chicken, or turkey

½ to ¾ cup shredded cheese (such as Cheddar, Monterey Jack, Swiss, or Feta)

1 teaspoon complementary dried herbs, or to taste

½ teaspoon salt, or to taste

FOR THE CUSTARD:
2½ cups milk

3 eggs, well beaten

1 large garlic clove, minced or 1 teaspoon garlic powder

2 tablespoons minced parsley

Before stratas or "impossible pies" appeared in every cookbook and on every dinner table, before quiches and frittatas graced every restaurant menu, Grandma made bread puddings: sweet puddings, savory puddings, endless combinations of bits of this and pieces of that, mixed with milk, eggs, and stale bread. Of admirable economy and great for breakfast, brunch, lunch, or dinner, bread puddings can be prepared ahead (in fact, are better when made ahead) and then baked when you are ready. They can sit overnight, covered, in the refrigerator for the next day's meal. Many can be served hot, warm, or cold and reheat nicely in the microwave. Starting with a basic formula that pretty much mirrored Grandma's recipe, we have over the years produced countless variations. The ingredients and proportions given here are general suggestions to be adapted to suit your taste. In addition to this basic recipe, on the adjacent page we've included two of our favorite savory bread puddings. (For your sweet tooth, also see the dessert section.)

Preheat the oven to 350° F. In a 1½-quart baking dish, lightly coated with cooking spray, distribute the bread cubes evenly and top them with the vegetables, meat, cheese, herbs, and salt. In a bowl combine the custard ingredients and gently pour the mixture into the baking dish. Let the mixture stand for at least 5 minutes for the bread to absorb some of the liquid then bake the pudding for 50 to 60 minutes, or until it is puffed, firm in the center, and a tester comes out clean. Serves 6 as a light brunch or lunch dish.

P&B's Hints: The bread pudding can be made, assembling all the ingredients in the baking dish and chilling the mixture, covered, up to one day in advance. Some of our favorite vegetable and herb combinations are as follows—asparagus with tarragon, broccoli with oregano, spinach with basil, and peas with marjoram.

SAVORY VEGETABLE BREAD PUDDINGS

MUSHROOM BREAD PUDDING

3 cups cubed rye bread

1 small onion, chopped

1 garlic clove, minced

8 ounces mushrooms, thinly sliced

½ teaspoon dried thyme

¼ teaspoon nutmeg

1 tablespoon butter

2¼ cups milk

3 eggs, well beaten

¼ cup sour cream

¾ teaspoon salt

2 tablespoons minced parsley

Preheat oven to 350° F. In a 2-quart baking dish, lightly coated with cooking spray, distribute the bread cubes evenly. In a skillet cook the onion, garlic, mushrooms, thyme, and nutmeg in the butter over moderate heat, stirring occasionally, until the mushrooms have released all their liquid and scatter the mixture evenly in the dish. In a bowl combine the milk, eggs, sour cream, salt, and parsley, gently pour the mixture into the dish, and let the mixture stand, stirring occasionally, for 5 minutes for the bread to absorb some of the liquid. Bake the pudding for 1 hour, or until it is firm in the center and a tester comes out clean. Serves 6 as a side dish with steak or roast meats.

ONION ROSEMARY BREAD PUDDING

3 cups cubed corn bread, preferably homemade

½ cup small-curd cottage cheese (plain or with chives)

1½ cups chopped onion

1 garlic clove, minced

2 teaspoons minced fresh rosemary or ¾ teaspoon dried

1 tablespoon butter

2½ cups milk

3 eggs, well beaten

¾ teaspoon salt

2 tablespoons minced parsley

Preheat oven to 350° F. In a 2-quart baking dish, lightly coated with cooking spray, distribute the bread cubes evenly and top them with scattered teaspoonfuls of cottage cheese. In a skillet cook the onion, garlic, and rosemary in the butter over moderate heat, stirring occasionally, until the onion is softened and scatter the mixture evenly in the dish. In a bowl combine the milk, eggs, salt, and parsley, gently pour the mixture into the baking dish, and let the mixture stand, stirring occasionally, for 5 minutes for the bread to absorb some of the liquid. Bake the pudding for 1 hour, or until it is firm in the center and a tester comes out clean. Serves 6 as a side dish with meat, poultry, or fish.

SAUTÉED ZUCCHINI PANCAKES

3½ cups scrubbed, trimmed, grated and loosely packed zucchini (about 1 pound)

¼ cup minced white part of scallion

⅓ cup freshly grated Parmesan

⅔ cup self-rising flour

1½ teaspoons minced fresh tarragon or ½ teaspoon dried

½ teaspoon salt

a big pinch of nutmeg

several grinds of fresh pepper

3 eggs

3 tablespoons mayonnaise

olive oil or butter for sautéing

your favorite homemade or store-bought salsa as an accompaniment

Anyone who has ever had a backyard vegetable garden knows that there comes a point in summer when the zucchini gets so out of control that, no matter how inventive you are, it is virtually impossible to use it all up—let alone give it away. Grandma and Mother did a better job than most in these endeavors, and this is just one of the ways they tackled the abundance. We've stuck closer to Grandma's recipe, which used whole eggs rather than Mother's egg substitute version, and added a topping of salsa to give the pancakes a little more zing.

    Squeeze handfuls of the zucchini well to remove most of the liquid, pat the zucchini dry on paper towels, and in a bowl combine it with the scallion, Parmesan, flour, tarragon, salt, nutmeg, and pepper. In a small bowl beat the eggs with the mayonnaise and stir the mixture into the zucchini mixture. In a large skillet cook heaping soup spoonfuls of the zucchini mixture (flattened slightly) in batches in 1 tablespoon oil over moderately high heat, adding more oil as necessary, until they are lightly browned on both sides. Transfer as the pancakes as they are done to a heated plate and serve them topped with salsa to taste. Serves 4 to 6.

P&B's Hints: Replace the tarragon with other fresh herbs such as dill, thyme, marjoram, or oregano (or use ½ teaspoon dried). Add ¼ cup minced red bell pepper for a more colorful dish.

OVERNIGHT BREAKFAST BAKE

Really an eggier version of bread pudding, this versatile all-in-one breakfast classic is easy to love. It appeals to almost everyone's tastes; but, for us, its most important attribute is that you can prepare it the night before. It's a great brunch dish and a lifesaver when you have houseguests and don't want to bother with making a fussy breakfast. For years, it was a Christmas tradition in our house. Mother quickly assembled the dish on Christmas Eve before we headed off to church services and the town's outdoor carol sing. The next morning we awoke early and opened our gifts—first things first—then, still dressed in robes and pajamas, we sat down to a lazy late breakfast that had baked while we were gathered round the tree. Mother made a pretty straightforward version, although we generally add a variety of culinary bells and whistles to the basics given here.

Scatter the bread cubes in an 8- by 12-inch baking dish, lightly coated with cooking spray. In a large bowl beat the eggs well and beat in the milk and the half-and-half along with the mustard and cornstarch (both dissolved in a little milk so that they don't lump), salt, and a few grinds of pepper. Stir in the Canadian bacon, cheese, and scallion, pour the mixture into the baking dish, distributing the solids evenly, and chill it, covered, overnight. Put the dish in a cold oven, set the temperature to 350° F., and bake the mixture for 45 minutes, or until it is puffed, lightly browned, and set in the center. Serves 6.

2 slices of slightly stale sandwich bread, dark crusts discarded and the bread cut into ½-inch cubes (about 1¾ cups)

6 extra-large eggs

1 cup fat-free milk

1 cup fat-free half-and-half

1½ teaspoons dried mustard

1 teaspoon cornstarch

½ teaspoon salt, or to taste

freshly ground pepper

¼ pound Canadian bacon, chopped coarse (about 1 cup)

1 cup low-fat grated sharp Cheddar or Monterey Jack cheese

¼ cup thinly sliced scallion

P&B's Hints: Create other combinations to suit your taste, substituting things like ham, crumbled cooked sausage or bacon, or diced smoked salmon to taste for the Canadian bacon, or using other vegetables such as chopped spinach, broccoli, or asparagus. We never warmed to the version Mother made with egg substitute to oblige our father's cardiologist, but we do use fat-free or low-fat dairy products, which you can replace with the richer stuff.

CHINESE-STYLE TOFU SAUTÉ

2 tablespoons soy sauce

1 tablespoon rice wine or medium-dry Sherry

2 teaspoons oyster sauce or hoisin sauce

½ teaspoon sugar

½ cup chicken or vegetable stock or broth

about 1 cup diced red bell pepper

about 1¼ cups diced zucchini

1 tablespoon peeled and minced gingerroot

1 large garlic clove, minced

1 tablespoon canola oil

1 teaspoon Asian sesame oil

½ teaspoon chili paste with garlic or hot bean sauce, or to taste

⅓ cup chopped scallion including the green tops

a 14-ounce package firm or extra-firm tofu, well drained and cut into ½-inch cubes

2 teaspoons cornstarch dissolved in ¼ cup water

minced cilantro to taste

steamed rice as an accompaniment

As far as we know, Grandma never encountered tofu. Were she ever asked about it, she most likely would have said it sounded like something you might name a small fluffy dog. Mother, however, had firsthand experience with various forms of bean curd during WWII when she worked as a nurse at a Japanese internment camp in California, where our army father was stationed. Although she learned to cook with it, tofu was not something that became part of our childhood diet, due in main to its lack of general availability, the era's lingering anti-Japanese sentiments, and Daddy's view that the spongy grayish lump didn't qualify as real food. In later years Mother began incorporating bean curd into Daddy's diet for health reasons, and even he came round to a grudging appreciation of its merits. The way we prepare tofu has its origin more in the Chinese home-style dish ma po bean curd, and we make it alternatively as a vegetarian dish or with meat (add ¼ pound sautéed ground pork or beef). This recipe is very flexible—proportions can be adjusted to taste preferences and any number of other vegetables can be added or substituted. These days tofu and the Chinese condiments we call for are routinely available in most large supermarkets.

In a small bowl combine the soy sauce, rice wine, oyster sauce, sugar, and chicken stock, stirring, until the sugar is dissolved. In a large skillet cook the red pepper, zucchini, ginger, and garlic in the oils over moderate heat, stirring occasionally, until they are softened slightly. Stir in the chili paste, then add the soy sauce mixture and cook the mixture, stirring occasionally, until it is heated through. Add the scallion and tofu and cook the mixture, tossing it together gently so as not to break up the tofu too much, until it is heated through. Drizzle the cornstarch mixture over the tofu mixture and continue to cook the mixture, tossing it together gently, until the sauce is thickened slightly. Sprinkle the tofu sauté with the cilantro and serve it with steamed rice. Serves 4.

SPIRITED CRANBERRY SAUCE

In our family, a long-standing controversy raged at Thanksgiving—over cranberry sauce. Grandma insisted on "the real thing," cooking down fresh cranberries with sugar syrup to a thick somewhat chunky sauce. We children wouldn't touch the stuff. Turned off by the residual chewy bits of skin and the bitter spikes of julienne orange rind she always added, we held out for the smooth, sweeter jellied sauce in a can. Daddy was in our camp on this one, Mother sided with Grandma, and Grandpa diplomatically laid low. So it was that both versions appeared on the table side by side in separate cut glass dishes. Grandma would surely be pleased to learn that we have subsequently come round to her side; and, though she might not openly approve, we think she would like our spirited adaptation of the real thing.

¾ cup lightly packed brown sugar

¾ cup Port wine

¼ cup Grand Marnier or triple sec

1 tablespoon grated orange rind

a 12-ounce package fresh cranberries, rinsed and picked over

In a nonreactive saucepan combine the sugar, Port, Grand Marnier, and rind and heat the mixture over moderate heat, stirring, until the sugar is dissolved. Add the cranberries and simmer the mixture, stirring occasionally, until the berries have popped and the sauce is thickened. Makes about 2 cups.

P&B's Hints: Some additions that we have incorporated at various times include cinnamon, chopped apple, minced candied ginger, currants/raisins, and chopped dried apricots. One year, when the Port and Grand Marnier were still packed away due to a move, we substituted some crème de cassis, and we still favor using it if we happen to have the spirit on hand.

PASTA, RICE, AND GRAINS

Both Grandma and Mother shared the view that every dinner meal should be constructed around three nutritional components: meat (poultry or fish counted here too), a vegetable of some sort, and what was referred to as "a starch." The proportions might vary depending on the situation, but most often the starch component—known casually today as carbs—dominated as it tended to be less expensive and served to fill us up best. Noodles, rice, and potato alternately shared the starring role, with biscuits or rolls filling in occasionally as understudies. We ate them all in large portions, the calories readily burned off through a more physically active life style. Old habits die hard, and, despite any anti-carb craze, we still like a starch with our dinner meals. Undoubtedly Grandma would be surprised to see just how far we've branched out from the basics, routinely including such things as kasha, quinoa, wild rice, bulgur, and couscous. The starch component in our dinner meals, however, is skewed in the opposite direction from Grandma's, playing instead a much smaller supporting role.

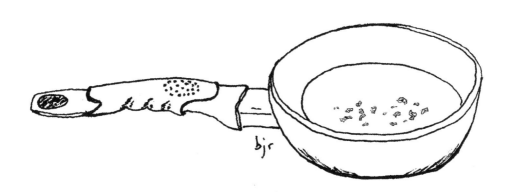

NOODLES WITH COTTAGE CHEESE AND HAM

1½ cups diced ham

1 tablespoon butter

12 ounces curly egg noodles, cooked al dente

⅓ cup minced chives or green part of scallion

1 teaspoon salt, or to taste

2 cups low-fat cottage cheese

buttered bread crumbs (page 111) as topping

Though our first inclination is to associate pasta with Italy, this noodle dish had its origins in Middle Europe, deriving from the Hungarian tarhonya, a rough egg-and-flour mixture that is grated and dried much like spaetzle. Grandma's version consisted of her own homemade spaetzle-like noodles and farmers cheese topped with buttered crumbs. True to his Hungarian roots, Grandpa proclaimed it one of his favorite supper dishes. Today we make our version with packaged curly egg noodles, low-fat cottage cheese, and chopped ham. Accompanied by a green salad, it is a simple light supper or lunch; but, more often, it turns up in our houses on the weekend breakfast table. We find the combination of tastes and textures—creamy cheese, salty nuggets of ham, tangy onion, and crisp crumb crunch—is in many ways more comforting and richly satisfying than fancier fare.

In a large skillet cook the ham in the butter over moderate heat, stirring, until it is lightly browned. Add the noodles, chives, and salt and cook the mixture, tossing it together lightly, until it is heated through. Dot the mixture with spoonfuls of the cottage cheese and toss it lightly and quickly until the cottage cheese is evenly distributed throughout the mixture and warmed but not fully melted. Serve the dish immediately, sprinkled with crisp buttered bread crumbs to taste. Serves 6.

P&B's Hints: Replace the chives with minced parsley, dill, or cilantro. Substitute crumbled cooked bacon, diced kielbasa, or other finely chopped cooked sausage for the ham. For faster last-minute preparation cook the noodles up to a day ahead and store them, covered and chilled.

PASTA WITH OVEN-ROASTED TOMATO SAUCE

Grandma was a living embodiment of Aesop's fable about the ant and the grasshopper as she toiled away canning, pickling, and preserving all summer long when garden produce was plentiful and cheap. Thus, come winter, her pantry shelves were lined with a bountiful supply of fruits and vegetables to see us through that lean season—including countless quart jars of stove-top simmered "stewed" tomatoes. Today, even though we are able to find fresh tomatoes year round, the wintertime grocery stock is a pretty sorry lot. This has led us to follow in Grandma's footsteps, capturing some of the special flavor of summer garden tomatoes in this rich sauce. We think that oven-roasting yields a mellower flavor than simmering does, and popping the sauce in the freezer sure beats the tedious business of canning. The sauce does wonders for a steaming bowl of pasta on a dreary February day.

Preheat the oven to 425° F. In a large bowl toss the tomatoes and reserved juice together with the onion, carrot, garlic, red pepper, herbs, sugar, and oil until the mixture is well combined. Transfer the mixture to a large, nonreactive rimmed baking sheet, arranging the pepper and tomato skin side up. Sprinkle the mixture generously with salt and pepper and roast it, stirring it around occasionally to prevent burning, for 45 minutes, or until the vegetables are soft. With tongs (or a knife) remove and discard the skins from the tomato and red pepper and in a food processor or blender process the mixture, juices and all, in batches if necessary, to the desired chunky or smooth texture. Serve the sauce over fettuccine or other pasta as a side dish and sprinkle the top with the Parmesan and additional fresh basil if desired. The sauce keeps, covered and chilled, for several days and can be frozen. Makes 3½ to 4 cups.

3½ pounds tomatoes, cored, halved horizontally, and seeded, reserving the juice

1 large onion, halved lengthwise and cut crosswise into ¼-inch slices (about 2 cups)

2 large carrots, trimmed and cut into ⅛-inch rounds (about 2 cups)

4 large garlic cloves, coarsely chopped

1 red bell pepper, quartered lengthwise, cored, and seeded

1 tablespoon chopped fresh basil, plus additional for garnish

2 teaspoons chopped fresh oregano or ½ teaspoon dried

a pinch of sugar

3 tablespoons extra virgin olive oil

pasta, cooked al dente

grated Parmesan to taste

SZECHWAN-STYLE SESAME NOODLES

1 small garlic clove, minced and mashed to a paste with ¼ teaspoon salt

1 tablespoon peeled and minced gingerroot

2 teaspoons Asian sesame oil

⅓ cup smooth peanut butter (or combine with part tahini)

1 tablespoon honey

¼ cup chicken broth or water

4 teaspoons rice vinegar or balsamic vinegar

2 tablespoons soy sauce

1 tablespoon hoisin sauce

½ pound spaghetti or linquine, cooked al dente, drained, and cooled

2 tablespoons minced scallion

2 tablespoon minced cilantro, or to taste

In Grandma's opinion peanut butter was chickadee or squirrel food and didn't qualify as human mealtime fare. Thus, PB&J was not a suitable sandwich for her grandchildren. Mother, however, wasn't about to stop making something that was universally kid-popular, easy to put together, and with more nutritional merit than, say, hot dogs and potato chips. So it is not surprising that when, in later years, we discovered Chinese food, our early addiction to peanut butter carried through to a special fondness for Szechwan-style peanut/sesame noodles. We love not only the taste of these noodles but also their ease of preparation and versatility in partnering with a variety of ingredients. Plus, we're pretty sure Grandma would give her nod of approval to this use of peanut butter.

In a nonreactive saucepan heat the garlic paste and ginger in the oil over moderately low heat, stirring, for 1 minute. Stir in the peanut butter, honey, broth, vinegar, soy sauce, and hoisin sauce and heat the mixture, stirring, until it is smooth. In a large bowl toss the noodles with the sauce, scallion, and cilantro. Serve the noodles warm, at room temperature, or chilled. Serves 4 as a side dish.

P&B's Hints: We often make these noodles into a main dish by adding various combinations of meat and vegetables. Chopped water chestnuts, celery, or cucumber or cooked snow peas, green peas, bell pepper, asparagus, or broccoli, plus chicken or pork, are some of our favored choices. If you like a bit of crunch, a sprinkling of chopped peanuts or toasted sesame seeds makes a good garnish. If, too, you have some of that garlic paste (page 125) on hand, this is a good place to use it in place of the minced and mashed garlic clove.

CLEAN-OUT-THE-FRIDGE FRIED RICE

As a young bride during WWII, Mother accompanied our father when he was stationed with the army in California and put her nursing skills to use in the Japanese internment camps. There she discovered soy sauce, and from then on this "exotic" condiment became a staple in her kitchen. During our childhood years Chinese-style food had just begun to appear in such Americanized dishes as chop suey, egg foo yung, and fried rice. Mother soon learned what Asians have long known, that fried rice is the ultimate in adaptability and an easy and tasty way to stretch food dollars. We have never made our fried rice exactly the same way twice, and every ten days or so we whip up a batch of it, tossing in all manner of leftovers from the refrigerator. This is a great way to use up the rest of that container of rice that came with your last Chinese takeout order, but, just to make certain there will be enough, we usually cook up an extra amount of plain rice so we always have a supply on hand. The recipe here is really an invitation to experiment—it's hard to go wrong.

⅔ cup diced red bell pepper

3 scallions including the green tops, chopped

2 garlic cloves, minced

2 teaspoons cooking oil such as canola

½ teaspoon Asian sesame oil

¾ cup diced ham

4 eggs, scrambled and coarsely chopped

¾ cup diced cooked green vegetables such as broccoli, cabbage, spinach, asparagus, or zucchini

4 to 5 cups leftover cold cooked rice

¼ cup soy sauce

2 tablespoons chicken broth

2 tablespoons minced cilantro

In a large skillet cook the red pepper, scallion, and garlic in the oils over moderately low heat, stirring, until they are softened slightly. Add the ham, egg, and green vegetable and cook the mixture until it is heated through. Add the rice, soy sauce, broth, 1 tablespoon of the cilantro, and salt to taste and toss the mixture together well. Cook the mixture, covered, tossing it together once halfway through, for 2 minutes, or until the rice is softened and the mixture is heated through. Sprinkle the fried rice with the remaining cilantro. Serves 4 to 6.

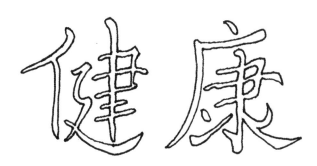

SPANGLISH RICE

1 cup long-grain rice

3 tablespoons olive oil or butter

1 cup chopped onion

¾ cup diced green bell pepper

¾ cup diced celery

1 tablespoon minced garlic

1 teaspoon salt

a 14-ounce can diced tomatoes with the juices

¾ cup chicken broth or water

Mother worked hard to serve food that fit into a tight budget but was, at the same time, nourishing and appetizing. One of the side dishes she made regularly was something she called Spanish rice, essentially rice flavored with canned tomatoes and a few herbs, which transformed plain white rice into something more interesting looking and tasting. The concept has stood the test of time, and these days we now make a slightly fancier version of her Spanish rice—a quick, easy, and flavorful accompaniment for a great variety of meat, chicken, or fish dishes.

In a large nonreactive saucepan cook the rice in the oil over moderately low heat, stirring occasionally, for 5 minutes. Add the onion, green pepper, celery, garlic, and salt and cook the mixture, stirring occasionally, until the vegetables are softened slightly. Add the tomatoes with their juices and the broth and simmer the mixture, covered, for 20 minutes, or until the liquid is absorbed. (Or, for easy oven to table serving, transfer the rice mixture to a 1½- to 2-quart casserole and cook it, covered, in a preheated 350° F. oven for 30 minutes, or until the liquid is absorbed.) Serves 6.

P&B's Hints: If we are in an Old World Spanish mood, we add ¼ teaspoon crumbled saffron to the dish; and, if it is a New World mood, we add about 1 tablespoon minced jalapeño pepper to the dish with the onion plus 1 tablespoon minced cilantro.

ORZO, WILD RICE, AND PECAN PILAF

On particularly steamy summer days a house without air conditioning was no place either Grandma or Mother wanted to cook a hot meal. Dinners of cold meat or chicken and a big salad were the usual answer. The salad generally contained a substantial starchy component, most often cold cooked potato, with leftover rice being next on the list. Over the years we have branched out from these confines thanks to a broader and more interesting selection of starchy ingredients. One of our favorite combinations these days is a hybrid salad/pilaf that marries the silken texture of orzo pasta with the slight chewiness of wild rice, complemented by nuts, dried fruit, and chopped vegetables and herbs. It is a great side dish to serve with grilled meat or poultry; and, if you add some chopped cooked chicken, it becomes a meal-in-one—perfect for a picnic.

In a large salad bowl toss together the orzo, wild rice, pecans, bell pepper, craisins, celery, parsley, and salt. In a small bowl beat together the oil, orange juice, vinegar, and mustard until the dressing is well combined. Pour the dressing over the wild rice mixture and toss the pilaf together, adding salt to taste if necessary, until it is well combined. Serve the pilaf at room temperature or chilled. The pilaf keeps, covered and chilled, for several days. Serves 8 to 10.

½ cup orzo, cooked al dente

¾ cup wild rice, cooked according to the package directions

¾ chopped pecans

¾ cup diced yellow or orange bell pepper

½ cup dried cranberries (craisins), cherries, or currants

½ cup thinly sliced celery

⅓ cup minced parsley or cilantro, or to taste

½ teaspoon salt, or to taste

⅓ cup extra virgin olive oil

¼ cup orange juice or apple cider

3 tablespoons balsamic vinegar

2 teaspoons Dijon-style mustard

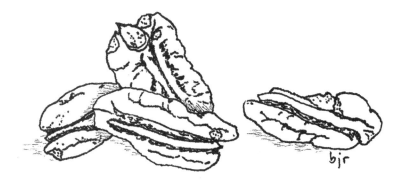

COCONUT CURRY QUINOA PILAF

2½ teaspoons curry powder

4 tablespoons mild olive oil

1 cup quinoa, rinsed well in cold water and drained well

1 teaspoon salt

1 cup finely chopped red onion

1 large garlic clove, minced

⅓ cup finely diced red bell pepper

1 cup finely diced zucchini

the juice of 1 lime

½ cup sweetened shredded coconut

2 tablespoons minced cilantro

¼ cup finely chopped, lightly toasted peanuts (optional)

If Grandma were to lay eyes on this recipe, she would be pretty much at a loss to picture it as a dish, imagine its taste, or even recognize the primary ingredient. Though one of the most ancient grains, quinoa is a fairly recent entry into today's grocery stores, part of a trend to resurrect heirloom plants and re-introduce them into the marketplace. High in protein, with a slightly nutty flavor, it is a versatile starchy accompaniment either on its own or in a pilaf like this one, which conveniently can be served warm, at room temperature, or chilled.

In a medium saucepan heat the curry powder in 3 tablespoons of the oil over moderate heat, stirring, to release the flavors and aroma. Stir in the quinoa and cook the mixture, stirring, for 2 minutes, or until the grains are well coated and the mixture is fragrant. Add 2 cups water and the salt and simmer the mixture, covered, for 10 minutes, or until the liquid is absorbed. Transfer the quinoa to a large bowl and let it cool slightly, fluffing it lightly with a fork to prevent it from lumping together. In a skillet cook the onion, garlic, red pepper, and zucchini in the remaining tablespoon oil over moderately low heat, stirring, until the vegetables are softened. Add the mixture to the quinoa with the lime juice, coconut, cilantro, and salt to taste, toss the pilaf together lightly until it is well combined, and sprinkle the top with the peanuts if desired. Serves 6.

P&B's Hints: For an even richer pilaf, use chicken broth instead of water. The pilaf reheats well in a skillet or microwave. Leftover pilaf, combined with chopped scrambled egg and ham, ranks high on our list of favorite off-beat breakfasts.

DRESSED-UP COUSCOUS

If Grandma were to sample a helping of plain couscous, that unknown substance would likely seem to her to be some bland and albino form of kasha (buckwheat groats). Or, it might appear to be a variation on the tiny pastina she routinely added to her chicken soup as a starchy filler. Generally available in a quick-cooking form, couscous is a staple in our pantries and a speedy means to fulfill Grandma's requirement that a well-rounded meal include a starch component. When there will be no accompanying sauce or gravy for the couscous, this is one of our favorite ways of dressing up its intrinsic blandness. The dish goes particularly well with grilled lamb, beef, or roast chicken.

3 cups chicken stock or broth, warmed

¼ teaspoon crumbled saffron threads

¾ cup currants

1½ cups finely chopped onion

2 garlic cloves, crushed and minced

4 teaspoons fruity olive oil

a 12-ounce package quick-cooking couscous, preferably whole-wheat

¼ cup minced cilantro or parsley

¼ cup pine nuts, lightly toasted

In a bowl or quart measuring cup pour the chicken stock over the saffron and the currants and let the mixture stand at least 10 minutes so that the saffron can soften slightly and the currants plump. In a saucepan cook the onion and garlic in the oil over moderately low heat, stirring, until they are softened slightly and stir in the stock mixture. Bring the stock to a boil, stir in the couscous, and simmer the mixture, covered, for 2 minutes. Let the couscous stand, covered, off the heat for 5 minutes, fluff it with a fork, and fold in the cilantro and the pine nuts. Serves 6.

P&B's Hints: The couscous can be prepared ahead without the cilantro and pine nuts and reheated in a microwaveable dish (add the cilantro and pine nuts after reheating). You could eliminate the pricey saffron, but it adds such a lovely subtle flavor and perfume that it's worth the investment.

SOUFFLÉED CHEESE GRITS

1 teaspoon salt

1 cup quick-cooking grits

4 tablespoons butter, cut into pieces

1 cup grated very sharp aged Cheddar

2 eggs

1 cup fat-free half-and-half

2 tablespoons grated Parmesan

To the best of our knowledge, Grandma never cooked or even had the experience of eating grits. We grew up eating cornmeal, and it was about as close as we came to grits until well after we left home and began to explore the world beyond New England. After traveling in the southeastern states and ultimately settling below the Mason-Dixon line, we have learned to appreciate a grain that we had previously written off as an uninteresting, coarser cousin to farina. We found, too, that many of the polenta-style dishes we had made with cornmeal could be modified for grits, and this is one of our favorite adaptations. If we've ever had any dinnertime leftovers, they've disappeared quickly—after a quick zap in the microwave—at the next morning's breakfast.

Preheat the oven to 350° F. In a saucepan bring 2½ cups water to a boil over high heat, add the salt and grits, and cook the mixture over moderate heat, stirring, for 3 minutes, or until it is very thick. Transfer the mixture to a large bowl, stir in the butter until it is melted, and stir in the cheese until it is melted. In a small bowl beat the eggs well with the half-and-half and stir the mixture into the grits mixture until the two are well combined. Transfer the mixture to a 2-quart soufflé dish, lightly coated with cooking spray, sprinkle the top with the Parmesan, and bake the grits mixture for 1 hour, or until the center is firm to the touch and a tester inserted in the center comes out relatively clean. Serves 6.

P&B's Hints: This recipe can serve as a backdrop for a number of flavorful additions such as crumbled cooked bacon, ground ham, chopped chile peppers, garlic, hot pepper sauce, mustard, minced scallion, shrimp, and, of course, chopped leftover pork barbecue.

CORNMEAL MUSH (POLENTA)

Hot cereal in some form or other was a breakfast fixture in our house, it being considered thrifty stick-to-your-ribs fare. Oatmeal was the regular offering along with the rhyming duo: farina and Wheatena. All of these were considered okay, but. when given a choice, we would always opt for the less frequently appearing cornmeal mush—made with yellow cornmeal and topped with browned butter and sugar or maple syrup. Cornmeal mush remains one of our favorite foods, but its role is now more often that of a side dish and its appearance has time-shifted to lunch or dinner. We serve it freshly made or we chill the cooked mush and serve it cut in slices and fried. The versions of cornmeal mush we make today are more adventurous than Mother's or Grandma's and usually incorporate a variety of tasty additions. Of course, we now have to call it polenta and serve it on the fancy china.

1½ cups yellow cornmeal

4½ cups chicken, beef, or vegetable broth or water

1 tablespoon butter or olive oil, plus additional for panfrying

½ teaspoon salt, or to taste

flour for dusting

In a bowl combine the cornmeal with 2½ cups of the broth. In a saucepan bring the remaining 2 cups broth to a boil and whisk in the cornmeal mixture, the 1 tablespoon butter, and the salt. Cook the mixture over moderately high heat, stirring, for 3 minutes, then reduce the heat and simmer the mixture, stirring often, for 20 minutes, or until it is thickened. (If you plan to make any of the additions noted below, now is the time to stir them in.) The polenta can be served, spooned out, at this point or you can pack it into a loaf pan, lightly coated with cooking spray, and chill it, covered with plastic wrap, until it is firm. The polenta keeps, covered and chilled, for several days. Cut the chilled polenta into ½-inch slices, dust the slices with flour, and in a large skillet panfry the slices in the additional butter until they are lightly browned on both sides and heated through. Serves 6.

A FEW THINGS WE LIKE TO ADD TO OUR POLENTA

- 1½ cups grated Cheddar and 1 teaspoon dry mustard
- ⅔ cup grated Parmesan and 1 tablespoon minced fresh thyme or oregano, or to taste
- 1 cup combined chopped cooked mushrooms, onions, and garlic
- 1 cup finely chopped ham or pepperoni or crumbled cooked bacon or Italian sausage
- 1¼ cups shredded Monterey Jack, 1½ tablespoons dried basil, 3 teaspoons chili powder, 2 teaspoons ground cumin, and 1 teaspoon garlic powder
- 1 cup combined minced scallion and your favorite herbs to taste

BREAD

When we were grade-schoolers, peanut butter and jelly on Wonder Bread was all the rage with our lunch-box crowd. Although supermarket bread was certainly the norm, both Grandma and Mother were of a mind that homemade bread was infinitely better tasting and better for you than the store-bought loaves. Mother regularly made a plain everyday loaf—something she called White Mountain—but what we really looked forward to were the days when she made oatmeal bread. It had an especially enticing aroma while baking, and the slightly swaybacked loaves had a rich nutty flavor with a hint of honey sweetness. If you love homemade bread and want to feed it to your children but have no time for producing hand-kneaded, twice-risen, oven-baked loaves, the bread machine is a wondrous invention. Through much experimenting with top-quality flours and grains, we have created machine bread that comes close in quality to oven-baked loaves. More importantly, however, the bread machine's programmable technology (simple enough that even we can figure it out) allows us to wake in the morning to the aroma of fresh bread and a just-baked loaf on the breakfast table. Incidentally, the machine also makes great pizza dough, which you can refrigerate or freeze. We have had good success in ordering specialty flours and other baking ingredients by mail from the Vermont-based King Arthur Flour company. The machine-made loaves on page 150 are two that we particularly enjoy, more so because Mother's oatmeal bread lives on in them.

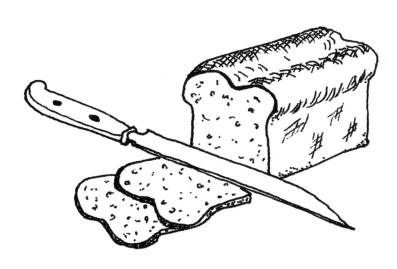

BREAD MACHINE BREADS

BARLEY OAT BREAD

1½ cups bread flour

½ cup barley flour (available at health food stores or by mail order)

¼ cup rolled oats (not instant or quick-cooking)

2 tablespoons wheat gluten (available at health foods stores or by mail order)

2 tablespoons powdered milk

2 tablespoons sesame seeds

1 tablespoon wheat germ (we like the crunchier toasted variety)

1 tablespoon oat bran

1¾ teaspoons active dry yeast

1 teaspoon salt

1 cup water

2 tablespoons honey

1 tablespoon vegetable oil

Add all of the ingredients to the baking pan of your bread machine in the order suggested in the machine's instruction manual. Bake the bread on a full-bake regular setting. The loaf may be time-baked. Makes a 1-pound loaf.

MAPLE OAT BREAD

2 cups unbleached all-purpose flour

½ cup whole-wheat flour

¾ cup rolled oats (not instant or quick-cooking)

¼ cup oat bran

1½ teaspoons active dry yeast

1 teaspoon salt

¾ cup water

½ cup maple syrup

2 tablespoons vegetable oil

Add all of the ingredients to the baking pan of your bread machine in the order suggested in the machine's instruction manual. Bake the bread on a full-bake regular setting. The loaf may be time-baked. Makes a 1½-pound loaf.

P&B's Hints: As a time-saver, we usually keep already mixed-up batches of the dry ingredients on hand in plastic containers so that they are ready to pop into the bread machine whenever a craving for fresh bread strikes.

BEER BREAD

Although no one in our family was much of a beer drinker, we really got into the voting for each year's Miss Rhinegold. (Daddy was always careful to pick a candidate with dark auburn hair like Mother's.) And, to this day, we can still sing the catchy jingle that advertised the beer. There was usually a bottle or two of lager in our refrigerator for a guest who might request it; but, with few takers, the beer usually ended up in a beef stew or a variation of this recipe. It's hard to find an easier bread to put together, and laziness is for once well rewarded. This hearty dense loaf keeps well and has a subtle malty flavor, making it a perfect partner for a ham and cheese sandwich spread with honey mustard. Sliced thin and trimmed into decorative shapes, the bread is also a great base for canapés.

Preheat the oven to 350° F. Into a bowl sift together the flours, sugar, baking powder, and salt. Stir in the beer, a third at a time, and combine the mixture well. The dough will be stiff and sticky. Transfer the dough to a 9- by 5-inch loaf pan, lightly coated with cooking spray, smooth the top, and bake the loaf for 45 minutes, or until it is lightly browned and a tester inserted in the center comes out clean. Turn the bread out onto a rack to cool and brush the top with melted butter, if desired, for a softer crust.

2 cups all-purpose flour

1 cup whole-wheat flour

3 tablespoon sugar, or to taste

1 tablespoon baking powder

½ teaspoon salt

a 12-ounce can or bottle of beer at room temperature

melted butter for brushing the loaf, if desired

ALMOST IRISH SODA BREAD

2 cups bread flour

1½ cups whole-wheat flour

½ cup quick-cooking oats

2 teaspoons baking powder

1 teaspoon baking soda

1 teaspoon salt

½ teaspoon ground caraway, if desired

8 ounces low-fat sour cream

¾ cup low-fat milk

¼ cup canola or other cooking oil

3 tablespoons sugar

½ cup currants, dusted with flour

Even Grandma didn't always have time to make the standard double-rising yeast loaves that usually filled her bread box, and a variety of quick breads in her repertoire came in handy on those occasions. This soda bread, perfect for weekend breakfast (delicious toasted too) or an afternoon snack, traces its origin to a recipe that an Irish neighbor shared with Grandma. Although many more traditional versions are made with buttermilk, we use low-fat sour cream, which imparts a similar tang along with a well-keeping quality.

Preheat the oven to 375° F. In a large bowl combine the flours, oats, baking powder, baking soda, and salt, plus the caraway if using. In another bowl combine the sour cream, milk, oil, and sugar. Add the sour cream mixture to the flour mixture with the currants and combine the dough well. Shape the dough into an 8-inch round, place it on a nonstick baking pan (or one lightly coated with cooking spray), and cut a ¾-inch-deep X across the top of the loaf. Bake the loaf for 40 minutes, or until it is browned and a tester inserted in the center comes out clean, and let it cool on a rack before slicing.

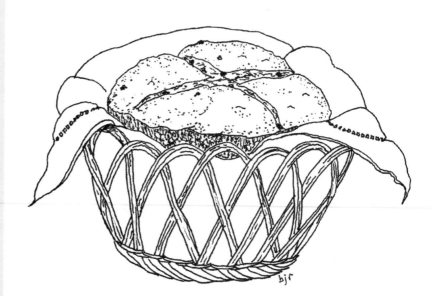

EASIEST-EVER BISCUITS

Mother always had something baking in the oven with wonderful aromas filling the entirety of our small house. Frequently it was a batch of biscuits, usually of the basic baking powder type. Making these involved cutting shortening into a flour mixture, then adding liquid to make a dough, which was either dropped by spoonfuls onto a baking sheet or patted out to the desired thickness and cut into rounds. Grandma's specialty was buttermilk biscuits, while Mother stuck to using plain milk and adding a bit of dry grated cheese. These days, especially in summer, we often throw together a big multi-ingredient salad for supper, and hot biscuits fresh from the oven are the perfect accompaniment. There's no fussy cutting shortening into the flour mixture (a procedure we never managed to get just right) in this ultra-simple, quick-cooking recipe. Delicate and fluffy, these biscuits also have none of the preservative taste we've found in the cardboard packaged versions in the grocery refrigerator case. We generally make an extra batch because the biscuits are also a great base for strawberry shortcake.

1 cup self-rising flour

¼ teaspoon baking soda

¼ teaspoon salt, or to taste

¾ cup full-fat sour cream

Preheat the oven to 450° F. In a bowl combine the flour, baking soda, and salt and stir in the sour cream to make a soft dough. Turn the dough out onto a lightly floured surface, knead it a couple of times, and pat it out ½ inch thick. Cut the dough into about 2-inch rounds with a biscuit cutter (a drinking glass or empty soup can works fine too) and arrange the biscuits on a baking sheet, lightly coated with cooking spray. Gather the dough scraps, kneading them together gently, pat them out as before, and cut out more biscuits. Bake the biscuits for 10 minutes, or until they have risen and are lightly browned. Makes about 10 biscuits.

P&B's Hints: For the super health-conscious, these can be made with low- or no-fat sour cream, though the texture will not be as light and delicate. Welcome flavor additions include: whatever herbs you like (dried work best, lavender adds a nice Provençal touch), grated cheese, bacon bits, minced baked ham, pepperoni, sun-dried tomato, and oil-cured olives. Biscuits cut slightly smaller make a good base for cocktail sandwiches. Cinnamon, nutmeg, and sugar are nice enhancements if the biscuits are to be used for shortcake.

APRICOT SCONES

3 cups flour

⅓ cup sugar, plus extra for sprinkling if desired

2½ teaspoons baking powder

1¼ teaspoons baking soda

¾ teaspoon salt

¼ teaspoon nutmeg

1½ sticks (¾ cup) cold butter, cut into 1-inch pieces

1¼ cups well-shaken fat-free buttermilk

½ cup finely chopped dried apricots, tossed in flour to separate the pieces

1 egg yolk, lightly beaten with 2 teaspoons water

Grandma loved buttermilk, drinking it with a gusto we reserve for a nicely oaked Chardonnay. Although certainly not to everyone's taste as a solitary glassful, buttermilk has no rival when it comes to imparting a lovely, fine moist crumb to many baked goods. There's always a carton of it in our refrigerators. Grandma made buttermilk biscuits; Mother made buttermilk muffins. We have combined the two conceptually (using fat-free instead of Grandma's full-fat buttermilk) and make these light and flaky scones. Various additions, listed below, make the scones useful for everything from breakfast, to snacks, to shortcake-style desserts.

Preheat the oven to 400° F. Into a bowl sift together the flour, sugar, baking powder, baking soda, salt, and nutmeg. Add the butter and incorporate it, rubbing the mixture together with your fingers until it resembles very coarse meal. Stir in the buttermilk and then the apricots until the dough is just combined. On a lightly floured surface knead the dough together very gently, halve it, and flatten each half into a ¾-inch-thick round. Cut each round into 8 wedges, brush each wedge lightly with the egg yolk mixture, and sprinkle the top lightly with sugar if desired. With a spatula transfer the wedges to a large baking sheet, lightly coated with cooking spray, leaving about an inch between them for expansion, and bake them for 15 minutes, or until they are puffed and lightly browned. Transfer the scones to a rack, let them cool slightly, and serve them warm. Makes 16 scones.

P&B's Hints: We have found any of these substitutions work well: ⅓ cup currants, raisins, dried cranberries, chopped dates, chopped walnuts or pecans, or even mini chocolate chips replacing the apricots. Or add flavorings such as ½ to ¾ teaspoon cinnamon, 1 tablespoon grated lemon or orange rind, or 1 teaspoon either vanilla or maple extract.

CINNAMON WALNUT SOUR CREAM COFFEECAKE

Ever practical, Grandma was always baking coffeecake, especially some version calling for sour milk or sour cream. Its multi-functionality made it useful for breakfast, brunch, a midmorning coffee break, an after-school snack, teatime, or—if plated up in a fancy manner—a simple dessert. Because it kept well it was a convenient thing to have on hand for serving drop-in guests at any time of the day or night. And, then too, it was easy to transport and thus perfect for a bake sale, potluck get-together, or church supper. Although our life style needs are different than Grandma's, we have found that a coffeecake habit dies hard, and we appreciate the make-ahead and long-keeping qualities of this delicious version. So forget about carbs, calories, and cholesterol and indulge in a slice.

½ cup finely ground walnuts or pecans

½ cup lightly packed brown sugar

2 teaspoons cinnamon

a large pinch of nutmeg

2 cups flour

1 teaspoons baking powder

½ teaspoon baking soda

1 stick (½ cup) butter, softened

¾ cup white sugar

2 eggs

1 teaspoon vanilla

8 ounces sour cream

Preheat the oven to 375° F. In a bowl combine the walnuts, brown sugar, cinnamon, and nutmeg. Into another bowl sift together the flour, baking powder, and baking soda. In a large bowl cream the butter with the white sugar until the mixture is smooth and beat in the eggs, one at a time. Add the vanilla and beat the mixture until it is light and fluffy and very pale in color. Gradually beat in the flour mixture alternately with the sour cream. Spoon a third of the batter into a 6-cup Bundt pan or tube pan, lightly coated with cooking spray, and top it with half of the walnut mixture. Layer the remaining batter and walnut mixture in the same manner, ending with a layer of batter, and bake the coffeecake for 55 minutes, or until it has pulled away slightly from the sides of the pan, is firm to the touch, and a tester inserted in the center comes out clean. Serves 6.

P&B's Hints: We have made this recipe variously with fat-free, low-fat, and full-fat sour cream. Taste- and texture-wise the results read in this order: good, better, best. Health-wise, of course, they read in reverse. All options work—your choice. One thing we particularly like is that the coffeecake can be prepared the night before, kept covered and chilled, and then baked the following morning for a great weekend breakfast (bake a refrigerated version about 5 minutes longer). The baked coffeecake also freezes well.

JAPAPEÑO CORN BREAD

1 cup yellow cornmeal

1 cup flour

2 tablespoons sugar

1½ teaspoons baking powder

½ teaspoon baking soda

1 teaspoon ground cumin

½ teaspoon salt

2 eggs

1 cup well-shaken buttermilk
(or ¾ cup buttermilk and ¼ cup
regular milk)

1 cup canned cream-style corn

4 tablespoons butter, melted

3 tablespoons minced sun-dried
tomato (optional)

1 cup grated sharp Cheddar or
Monterey Jack

½ cup diced jalapeño peppers
(about a 4-ounce can, drained),
or milder chile peppers to taste

¼ cup crumbled crisp-cooked
bacon

Back when Grandma and Mother were whipping up batches of corn bread at least once a week, there were two basic schools of thought regarding how this American specialty was made: northern and southern. It was all about color and texture. Northern meant yellow cornmeal and a fluffier, cakier quality, whereas southern meant white cornmeal and a denser consistency with a crisper crust. As New Englanders, we were in the northern camp. The corn breads we make now have branched out from Grandma's Puritan plain version, and they lean toward the Southwest in sensibility. Almost creamy in texture and full of flavorful additions, this version is almost a meal in itself. We use stone-ground cornmeal when we can find it as it gives a richer, nuttier taste than the mass-produced machine-milled products.

Preheat the oven to 425° F. Into a bowl sift together the cornmeal, flour, sugar, baking powder, baking soda, cumin, and salt. In a large bowl beat the eggs well and stir in the buttermilk, creamed corn, melted butter, and sun-dried tomato if using. Stir the flour mixture into the egg mixture until the batter is just combined. Fold in the cheese, chiles, and bacon and pour the batter into a 9-inch-square baking pan, well coated with cooking spray. Bake the corn bread for 25 minutes, or until the top is lightly browned, the sides have pulled away from the edge of the pan slightly, and a tester inserted in the center comes out clean. Let the corn bread cool in the pan on a rack for 5 minutes before slicing and serve it warm. Serves 6 to 8.

P&B's Hints: If using fresh chiles, be sure to wear rubber gloves to protect hands from the stinging oils while chopping. Chorizo or pepperoni, minced or finely chopped in the food processor, can be substituted for the bacon. The bread can be reheated in the pan, covered with foil, in a 350° F. oven for 10 to 15 minutes.

BUTTERMILK HONEY CORN BREAD

Our favorite simple corn bread is made with buttermilk and honey. It is slightly more refined than homier versions, with a lovely smooth texture, and, best of all, it is very quick and easy to put together. The buttermilk imparts a wonderful moistness, so that the corn bread keeps well.

Preheat the oven to 425° F. In a bowl whisk together the cornmeal, flour, baking powder, and salt. In another bowl beat together the eggs, buttermilk, and honey. Stir the flour mixture into the egg mixture, stir in the melted butter, and combine the batter well. Pour the batter into an 8-inch-square baking pan, lightly coated with cooking spray, and bake the corn bread for 30 minutes, or until it is lightly browned, the edges pull away from the sides of the pan, and a tester inserted in the center comes out clean. Serve the corn bread warm. Serves 6.

1¼ cups yellow cornmeal

¾ cup flour

2 teaspoons baking powder

½ teaspoon salt

2 eggs

1¼ cups well-shaken buttermilk

¼ cup honey, or to taste

4 tablespoons butter, melted

ENGLISH MUFFIN PIZZA

4 English muffins (we prefer the taste and texture of the Thomas' brand), separated into halves

8 slices mozzarella cheese, about ¼ inch thick and trimmed to fit the muffin halves

about 1½ cups your favorite homemade or store-bought tomato sauce (we often use leftover spaghetti sauce) or seeded and finely chopped fresh tomato

a combination of your favorite pizza toppings such as finely chopped cooked Italian sausage, bacon, ground beef, or chicken, or thinly sliced pepperoni or onions, or chopped green bell pepper, anchovies, mushrooms, or leftover cooked vegetables such as broccoli or spinach

chopped fresh basil or oregano (optional)

When we were young children, about the only place to get pizza was an Italian family-run eatery connected to a tavern in the neighboring town, and it was Grandpa who always went and procured the pizza as a treat for us. Grandma and Mother had suspicions that the real reason for these forays was not just to win the affection of his grandchildren but because the tavern was also the nearest place where he could bet on the horses. To pacify us between Grandpa's pizza runs, Mother came up with the following homemade substitute, which we could assemble and cook ourselves. Over the years we have adapted and internationalized her basic preparation. It provides a quick and satisfying pizza fix in less time than it would take for the delivery man to arrive with your takeout order.

Toast the muffin halves lightly to crisp them slightly and arrange them, center side up, on a baking sheet. Top the halves with the cheese slices (eat the trimmings), spread the tomato on the cheese, and add your choice of toppings. Cook the mini pizzas under a preheated broiler or in a preheated 400° F. oven or toaster oven (watch them carefully) until the cheese is melted and lightly colored and the toppings are heated through. Transfer the pizzas to serving plates with a spatula. Serves 4.

P&B's Hints: Some of our favorite combinations are Tex-Mex: with Monterey Jack cheese, salsa, chile peppers, and a sprinkling of cilantro; Spanish-style: with Manchego cheese, chorizo, and pimiento peppers or red pepper purée; Continental: with a bit of mustard spread on the muffin and topped with Brie cheese and chopped Black Forest ham; Chinese: with chopped barbecued pork and a touch of hoisin sauce and sprinkling of cilantro.

MUFFINS

From rustically simple to multi-flavored, muffins in some form were almost as common as toast on our breakfast table. Using a recipe she learned at Grandma's apron-covered knee, Mother could whip up a batch of muffins, plus make coffee and set the breakfast table, in less time than it took to preheat the oven in our huge old gas stove. Twenty minutes or so later, golden muffins would be ready to devour, spread with homemade jam. For special occasions, a sprinkling of cinnamon sugar would crown the top of each muffin with a sweet, crispy coating. Over the years we have added countless variations to the basic recipe—all a lasting tribute to the goodness of the original. They're so easy you can try them all and also create your own combinations. And, remember, muffins aren't just for breakfast anymore!

KEY TO SUCCESS: The key to successful muffins is two-fold. First and foremost: Use the quickest and lightest touch when mixing the wet and dry ingredients. The batter should be minimally combined. It is just right when it is thick and lumpy and you can still see some flour. Second: Resist the temptation to open the oven door to check on the muffins' progress. Let them have at least the suggested baking time before you peek. Most will probably need some extra minutes, depending on what additions have been made to the basic batter.

BASIC MUFFINS

1 egg

1 cup milk

¾ cup mild vegetable oil

½ teaspoon vanilla

2 cups sifted flour

¼ to ⅓ cup sugar

3 teaspoons baking powder

½ teaspoon salt

The following recipe is our "little black dress" in the realm of muffin couture. It is a lovely simple muffin by itself, plus it serves as the basis for countless additional sweet and—minus some of the sugar—savory variations. See the adjacent page for some of our favorite flavorings.

Preheat the oven to 400° F. In a bowl beat together the egg, milk, oil, and vanilla. Into another bowl sift together the flour, sugar, baking powder, and salt. Add the dry ingredients to the wet ingredients and stir the mixture together quickly and very gently until it is just barely combined. Fill muffin cups, lightly coated with cooking spray, ¾ full and bake the muffins for 20 minutes, or until they are lightly browned and a tester inserted in the center comes out clean. Makes 12 medium-sized muffins.

P&B's Hints: Plan ahead and do most of the preparation up to 12 hours in advance. Mix the dry ingredients together and set them aside, covered. Mix the wet ingredients together and reserve them, covered and chilled. Nuts, herbs, raisins or dried fruit can be mixed in with the dry ingredients. Items such as applesauce, cooked mushrooms, grated rinds, or syrups and flavorings can be added to the egg/milk/oil mixture. Ingredients such as cheese, meats, and fresh fruits are best kept refrigerated separately and folded in just before baking.

MANY-LIVED MUFFINS

- ⅓ to ½ cup finely chopped nuts and 1 tablespoon molasses or maple syrup
- ⅓ to ½ cup currants or raisins, 1 teaspoon cinnamon, and sprinkle tops with cinnamon sugar (page 174)
- 1 peeled and chopped apple, 1 teaspoon cinnamon, and sprinkle tops with cinnamon sugar (page 174)
- ¼ cup applesauce and 1 teaspoon cinnamon
- ⅓ cup well-drained crushed pineapple
- ¼ cup finely chopped crystallized ginger
- ½ cup any finely chopped dried fruit (apricots, mangoes, cranberries, dates, etc.)
- ½ cup mashed ripe banana
- 1 cup fresh small blueberries
- 1 tablespoon grated lemon rind or orange rind
- For Swedish limpa muffins add 1 tablespoon molasses, 1 tablespoon grated orange rind, and 1 tablespoon slightly crushed fennel, caraway, or anise seeds (or a combination).

SAVORY ADDITIONS
(Reduce the sugar to 2 tablespoons and eliminate the vanilla)

- ¾ cup shredded cheese (any kind)
- 1 tablespoon dried herbes de Provence
- ½ cup minced ham and 1½ teaspoons dried mustard
- ½ cup crumbled cooked bacon
- ¼ cup finely chopped pepperoni
- ½ cup cooked finely chopped mushrooms and onions and 1 teaspoon dried thyme
- 2 tablespoons grated Parmesan, 1 tablespoon dried oregano, and 1 teaspoon garlic powder
- ¼ cup chopped oil-cured black olives and 1 tablespoon minced fresh rosemary (or 1 teaspoon ground dried)
- ½ cup finely chopped cooked Italian sausage and 1 tablespoon dried basil or sage
- For chili corn muffins replace 1 cup of the flour with 1 cup yellow cornmeal, up the salt to ¾ teaspoon, and add ¾ cup shredded Cheddar or Monterey Jack (with or without jalapeño), 1 tablespoon chile powder, and 1 teaspoon ground cumin.

REFRIGERATOR RAISIN BRAN MUFFINS

2 eggs

2 cups well-shaken buttermilk

⅓ cup vegetable oil (preferably canola)

1 tablespoon grated orange rind

2½ cups flour

1 cup lightly packed light brown sugar

3 teaspoons baking soda

2 teaspoons ground ginger

1 teaspoon cinnamon or 5-spice powder

1 teaspoon salt

3½ cups raisin bran cereal

As each new generation of housewives strayed farther from hearth and home and cooking from scratch, the concept of make-ahead became a rallying cry. By the 1940s almost every cookbook had recipes for batters or doughs that could be prepared ahead of time and refrigerated for later baking into muffins or cookies that would thus be "ready in a jiffy." We don't know where Mother's refrigerator bran muffin recipe came from originally, but it has gone through numerous incarnations as we have added or substituted ingredients without abandoning the make-ahead approach. Although we rarely prepare the batter exactly the same way, the basic recipe here serves as our jumping off point.

In a bowl beat together the eggs, buttermilk, oil, and rind. Into a large bowl sift together the flour, sugar, baking soda, ginger, cinnamon, and salt and stir in the raisin bran cereal. Add the buttermilk mixture to the flour mixture and fold the batter together gently until it is just combined. At this point the batter may be stored in a sealed container in the refrigerator for up to 6 weeks (see Hints below). Preheat the oven to 400° F. (425° F. if using a toaster oven for 3 or fewer muffins in custard cups). Coat the muffin tins or cups lightly with cooking spray, fill them ⅔ full with batter, and bake the muffins until they are firm on top and a tester inserted in the center comes out clean. The baking time will be about 25 minutes for muffins in regular muffin tins, 20 minutes if in custard cups, and 10 minutes if in mini muffin tins. Makes about 5 cups of batter.

P&B's Hints: Put a piece of tape on the batter container with the date on it. Weeks can fly by, and it would be a shame to have even a drop of this yummy batter not grow into a muffin.

TOMORROW MORNING OATMEAL PANCAKES

Breakfast favorites such as pancakes tended to be weekend fare in our house, as there usually wasn't time before school to whip up these things, let alone eat them at a leisurely pace. Similar time constraints have stayed with us over the years as we graduated from being students to workers. Taking ideas from an old Irish recipe for make-ahead oatmeal, soaked overnight in cream, and one of Mother's refrigerator muffin recipes, we experimented and created this overnight pancake preparation. With the batter already made, these pancakes are a quick enough breakfast for weekday as well as weekend enjoyment.

In a bowl beat together the eggs, oil, honey, vanilla, and buttermilk. Stir in the oats, flour, sugar, baking soda, cinnamon, and nutmeg, and chill the mixture, covered with plastic wrap, overnight. Stir the batter once and cook ¼ cups of it on a nonstick griddle (or one lightly coated with cooking spray) over moderately high heat until both sides are lightly browned. Serves 4.

2 eggs

1 tablespoon vegetable oil (preferably canola)

1 tablespoon honey

1 teaspoon vanilla

2 cups well-shaken buttermilk

1½ cups regular rolled oats (not instant or quick-cooking)

¾ cup flour

1 tablespoon brown sugar

1 teaspoon baking soda

½ teaspoon cinnamon, or to taste

a pinch of nutmeg

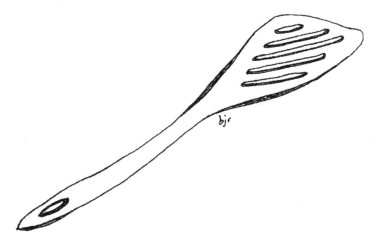

P&B's Hints: We usually add blueberries to these pancakes, and, when they are not in season, we add grated apple. The batter works just fine with fat-free buttermilk if you want to off-load a few fat grams or calories. Rather than employing the make-ahead procedure, if you want to make a batch of pancakes right away, substitute instant oatmeal for the regular.

SOUFFLÉED APPLE PANCAKE

1 small tart cooking apple

1 tablespoon lemon juice

2 tablespoons sugar combined with ¼ teaspoon cinnamon

2 extra-large eggs

6 tablespoons milk

6 tablespoons flour

a pinch of salt

a pinch of nutmeg

This fruit-studded, slightly sweet first cousin to popovers was one the many ways both Grandma and Mother used their ingenuity to produce dishes that appeared fancy but were made quickly and easily with inexpensive everyday staples. We eat this puffed pancake, drenched in maple syrup, for Saturday or Sunday breakfast with ham steak or homemade sausage patties. We have also enjoyed it as a dessert, topped with vanilla ice cream and caramel or chocolate sauce. Thinly sliced pear, Chinese pear-apple, or even quince make nice flavor variations in place of the apple.

Preheat the oven to 425° F. Quarter the apple lengthwise, then peel, core, and cut it into very thin slices. In a small nonreactive bowl toss the apple slices with the lemon juice and 1 tablespoon of the cinnamon sugar. In another bowl whisk together the eggs and milk, add the flour, salt, and nutmeg, and stir the batter until it is just combined. The batter will be lumpy. Pour the batter into a 9-inch pie plate, lightly coated with cooking spray, evenly distribute the apple slices on top, and sprinkle the remaining tablespoon of cinnamon sugar over the mixture. Bake the pancake for 15 minutes, or until it is well puffed and golden brown, and serve it immediately. Serves 2 to 4.

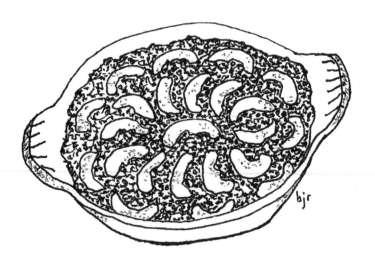

POPOVERS

Grandma's secret to making popovers that were high rising, crisp on the outside, and moist on the inside was to mix the batter lightly until it was just combined and bake it in a sizzlingly hot cast iron pan in a very hot oven. We still have the heavy black monster that she and Mother used: a dozen deep cast iron cups fused together at the rims. It makes matchless popovers. It is also awkward to use, cumbersome to clean, and overly large for our everyday needs. When pressed for time and we crave just a couple popovers for breakfast or a Yorkshire pudding-style accompaniment to roast beef, this short-cut recipe is a great solution. Although standard muffin tins or custard cups don't produce as perfect popovers as Grandma's special pan, they do a pretty fine job and more than make up for the slight qualitative lapse with their greater ease and efficiency.

1 extra-large egg at room temperature

½ cup milk, warmed slightly

½ cup sifted all-purpose flour

a pinch of nutmeg

¼ teaspoon salt

Put a baking sheet in the lower third of the oven and preheat the oven to 425° F. In a bowl whisk together the egg and milk and gently stir in the flour, nutmeg, and salt until the batter is just combined. Divide the batter among either 4 cups of a muffin tin or 4 custard cups, all well coated with cooking spray. Set the tin or cups on the baking sheet in the oven and bake the popovers for 15 minutes. Reduce the heat to 350° F. and bake the popovers for 10 minutes more, or until they are well puffed and golden brown. Stab the top of each popover with a sharp knife, let the popovers stand in the oven for a few minutes to release the steam, and serve them at once. Makes 4 popovers.

P&B's Hints: The recipe can be increased proportionally to meet your needs. It also works better if the muffin tins are not of nonstick material. If the popovers are going to be served with chicken, try adding ¼ teaspoon each of garlic powder and dried thyme to the batter. With lamb or pork, ¼ teaspoon each of garlic powder and crumbled dried rosemary are nice additions.

SWEETS

Without fail, Mother served dessert with dinner every night. She was savvy enough to know that holding out the carrot of a sweet at the end of the meal was the best way to make sure we ate the more nutritious, usually less appealing, fare that preceded it. With a focus on economy, dessert was usually concocted from basic household staples plus some sort of seasonal fruit when it could be conveniently incorporated. There were puddings, pies, and cookies galore, and then there was cake. In our house "cake" fell into several different categories. The most exalted of these was birthday-cake style: a multilayer production separated with a puddingy filling and covered with a confectioners' sugar type of frosting. Grandma's made-from-scratch coconut cake was the winner in this category. Although Mother continued the tradition by making Daddy's favorite Lady Baltimore cake, Duncan Hines gradually took over on most occasions. Moving down the hierarchy came a few specialty cakes such as angel food and gingerbread, followed by the pound cake family, and then the coffeecake group. Though we have a sweet tooth that wanders far and wide these days, we reserve a special fondness for cakes and are constantly tinkering with, as well as adding to, the extensive collection of them handed down from Grandma and Mother.

CHOCOLATE ALMOND TORTE

¼ cup chopped dried cherries or whole currants

¼ cup Scotch whisky or Cognac or Armagnac

3 ounces blanched slivered almonds (about ⅔ cup), very finely ground in a food processor

4½ tablespoons cake flour

4 ounces semisweet chocolate

3 ounces sweet chocolate

½ teaspoon instant coffee granules

1 stick (½ cup) butter, softened

⅔ cup sugar

3 egg yolks

4 egg whites

flour and confectioners' sugar for dusting

The special fondness for cake that we developed early in life continues to evolve, and we currently tend to favor a single-layer torte style, often with a fruit or nut component. Thus, when a chocolate craving strikes we find ourselves making some version of this rich torte, which includes both fruit and nuts and marries the spirit of Grandma's rich nut-based pastries with that of an early Simone Beck French chocolate cake.

In a small bowl let the cherries or currants soak in the whisky until they are softened slightly. In another small bowl combine the ground almonds and cake flour. Preheat the oven to 375° F. In a microwaveable bowl melt the chocolates with 3 tablespoons water and the coffee in the microwave, stirring occasionally, until the mixture is smooth. Stir in the butter, a little at a time, until the mixture is well combined. In a large bowl beat the sugar with the yolks until the mixture is very pale in color and stir in the chocolate mixture followed by the almond mixture and the cherries and liquor. In another bowl beat the egg whites with a pinch of salt until they hold stiff peaks. Gently stir a third of the whites into the batter to lighten it and then gently fold in the remaining whites. Transfer the batter to an 8½-inch springform pan, lightly coated with cooking spray and dusted with flour, and bake the torte in the center of the oven for 20 minutes, or until it is firm on the outside edges but still slightly soft in the center. Let the cake cool in the pan on a rack for 15 minutes then remove it from the pan and let it cool completely on the rack. Dust the torte lightly with confectioners' sugar just before serving. The cake is so rich it easily serves 8 to 10.

P&B's Hints: When we want the dessert to look extra fancy, we serve slices of the torte on a bed of sauce made with puréed strawberries and raspberries and top each serving with a mint leaf.

APPLE-PEAR PECAN TORTE

This simple, not-too-sweet nut torte is almost a coffeecake or tea cake and has sat as often on the brunch table as on a dessert plate in our houses. It is reminiscent of Grandma's buttery rich Austro-Hungarian nut torte in taste, but it is far easier to make. Though it is by no means dietetic fare, the fruit allows us to feel more virtuous health-wise.

Preheat the oven to 350° F. Into a small bowl sift together the flour, baking powder, baking soda, and cinnamon. In a larger bowl beat the eggs with the sugar and vanilla until the mixture is thick and very pale in color then stir in the flour mixture followed by the pecans, apple, and pear until the batter is well combined. Transfer the batter to an 8-inch springform pan, lightly coated with cooking spray, and bake the torte for 25 minutes, or until it pulls away slightly from the sides of the pan, is springy to the touch, and a tester inserted in the center comes out clean. Let the torte cool slightly in the pan on a rack before removing it from the pan. Dust the cake with confectioners' sugar just before serving. Serves 8.

¼ cup flour

1 teaspoon baking powder

a pinch of baking soda

¼ teaspoon cinnamon

2 eggs

⅓ cup lightly packed light brown sugar

1½ teaspoons vanilla

1¼ cups pecans, finely ground

½ cup peeled, cored, and grated apple

½ cup peeled, cored, and grated firm Bosc pear

confectioners' sugar for dusting

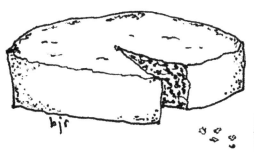

P&B's Hints: We often make this versatile torte with other nuts, especially walnuts or hazelnuts, and with all apple or pear or with quince or Asian pear-apple. Ground ginger and five-spice powder are also nice substitutions for the cinnamon. Though it's far better fresh baked, you can freeze the torte.

PICK-A-FLAVOR TEA CAKES

4 cups flour

1 teaspoon baking powder

1 teaspoon salt

4 sticks (1 pound) butter, softened

2½ cups sugar

8 eggs

½ cup fat-free half-and-half

2 teaspoons vanilla

Grandma never arrived to visit anyone empty-handed, nor did anyone who visited her leave empty-handed (or empty-stomached!). Favored among the foodstuffs she bestowed on all were what she called tea cakes, delectably butter-rich small loaves, flavored with whatever she might have on hand. It is a tradition that has endured in our family. We love baking up a batch of these mini loaves—essentially pound cakes—deciding what flavor suits our mood or what we think might best please the person to whom the loaf will be going. Although the basic batter recipe has remained pretty much unchanged through the years, some of our flavor additions would surely shake up Grandma's taste buds.

Before you start the batter, set aside 7 flavorings (such as those listed on the adjacent page or others of your own choosing) and portion them out individually so that they may be stirred into each separate portion of cake batter. Into a bowl sift together the flour, baking powder, and salt. In a large bowl with a mixer cream together the butter and sugar until the mixture is light and fluffy. Add the eggs, one at a time, beating well after each addition, and beat the mixture until it is smooth. Beat in the half-and-half and vanilla. Beat the flour mixture into the butter mixture, a little at a time, until it is fully incorporated. Preheat the oven to 375° F. Divide the batter evenly among 7 small bowls, using about 1¼ cups per bowl, and add to each bowl the individual flavoring selections. Transfer the flavored batters to mini loaf pans (about 5¾ by 3¼ by 2 inches), lightly coated with cooking spray, and bake the loaves for 30 minutes, or until they are lightly browned, the edges have pulled away slightly from the sides of the pan, and a tester inserted in the center comes out clean. Let the loaves cool in the pans on racks for 15 minutes, then turn them out onto the racks to cool completely. Makes 7 tea cakes.

P&B's Hints: The tea cakes freeze well. They can be dusted with confectioners' sugar or topped with a simple icing of your choosing. The plain tea cakes make a nice base for shortcake. The batter can also be baked in various larger size loaf or tube pans, filling the pans no more than two-thirds full and adjusting the baking times upward.

A SELECTION OF TEA CAKE FLAVORINGS

- ¼ cup finely chopped walnuts and ½ teaspoon maple extract

- 1 teaspoon grated lemon rind and 1 teaspoon lemon juice

- ½ teaspoon rum extract and ¼ cup currants

- 1 teaspoon orange rind and 1 teaspoon triple sec

- ¼ cup chopped dried apricots, dusted with flour, and ¼ teaspoon ground cardamom

- 2 tablespoons minced candied ginger, dusted with flour, and ¼ teaspoon powdered ginger

- 1 teaspoon instant coffee granules and ¼ cup mini chocolate chips

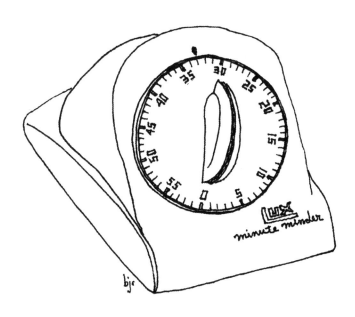

GRANDMA'S GINGERBREAD

¾ cup light molasses

2½ cups flour

2 teaspoons baking soda

2 teaspoons ground ginger

½ teaspoon cinnamon

¼ teaspoon ground allspice

¼ teaspoon ground clove

½ teaspoon salt

1 stick (½ cup) butter, softened

½ cup lightly packed dark brown sugar

½ cup white sugar

2 large eggs

lemon dessert sauce (adjacent page) as an accompaniment

We grew up on gingerbread. In this heyday of crème brulée, tiramisù, and baklava, there is something almost sweetly naïve about this spice cake, an old-fashioned country girl lost in a crowd of cosmopolitan sophisticates. Gingerbread is not something you expect to encounter on a restaurant menu, be served at a dinner party, or find in the supermarket bakery case. But, on a dreary cold day when we are feeling less than cheery, few things are as spirit boosting as the rich fragrance of a pan of it baking and the satisfying comfort of its spicy sweet taste set off with a silky, tart lemon sauce. Thus, it is one of the few family recipes that have survived pretty much tamper-free over the years.

Preheat the oven to 350° F. In a small bowl combine the molasses with ¾ cup boiling water. Into a bowl sift together the flour, baking soda, ginger, cinnamon, allspice, clove, and salt. In a large bowl with a mixer cream together the butter and sugars until the mixture is light and fluffy, add the eggs, and beat the mixture well. Gradually beat in the flour mixture and then stir in the molasses mixture, stirring until the batter is smooth. Pour the batter into a 9-inch-square baking pan, lightly coated with cooking spray and dusted with flour, and bake it for 35 minutes, or until the edges begin to pull away from the sides of the pan and a tester inserted in the center comes out clean. Let the gingerbread cool in the pan for 5 minutes, turn it out onto a rack, and serve it warm with lemon dessert sauce. Serves 6 to 8.

LEMON DESSERT SAUCE

Although the gingerbread we had at friends' houses generally had either a sugary nut crust or cream cheese frosting, Grandma and Mother always served ours with a simple lemon (or lemon-lime) sauce. We maintain that tradition because the sauce is ridiculously easy to make and its versatility extends well beyond merely accompanying gingerbread. It's great spooned over plain yogurt or vanilla ice cream and can provide a refreshing take on summer shortcake: top pound cake, angel food cake, or a sweet biscuit with vanilla ice cream, blueberries, and some of the sauce.

In a nonreactive saucepan combine the sugar, cornstarch, and salt. Whisk in 1½ cups boiling water and cook the mixture over moderate heat, stirring, for 3 minutes, or until the sugar is dissolved and the sauce is thickened and smooth. Remove the pan from the heat and stir in the lemon juice and rind. Serve the sauce hot or cold. Makes about 2 cups.

1 cup sugar

2 tablespoons cornstarch

a pinch of salt

½ cup fresh lemon juice (or a lemon-lime combination)

2 teaspoons grated lemon rind

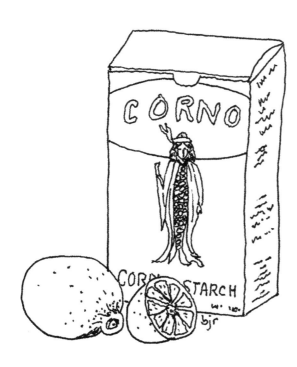

CINNAMON SUGAR

1 to 2 teaspoons cinnamon

½ cup granulated sugar

NOTE: Our favorite variant is cardamom sugar—substitute 1 to 2 teaspoons ground cardamom for the cinnamon

Cinnamon was a mainstay in Mother's baking repertoire, even more than it was in Grandma's. All of the spices in our house were stored, stacked three or four atop one another, in the deep bottom drawer of a small kitchen worktable. The drawer was peevishly temperamental, heavy, and prone to sticking unless pulled out at just the right angle. Although only Mother was able to find things in there—following some personal spice-country map stored in her head—we knew that cinnamon was always handy, front and center on the top of the pile. Alongside the store-bought sticks and powdered cinnamon was a shaker-topped glass jar containing cinnamon sugar, which Mother regularly mixed up for adding sweet spiciness to everything from oatmeal to apple crisp, coffeecake to simple buttered toast. A similar jar now sits in our spice cabinets as well.

In a small bowl stir ½ teaspoon of the cinnamon into the sugar until the mixture is well combined. Gradually stir in more of the cinnamon, tasting the mixture as you go along, until the desired strength is reached. Store the cinnamon sugar sealed in a glass jar. Keeps indefinitely.

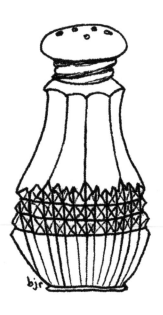

SWEETISH SWEDISH BLUEBERRY CAKE

Our first experience with blueberries was nibbling the fruit from the few berry bushes that grew in Grandma's backyard, and it was love at first bite. With wily netting, Grandma somehow managed to thwart the resident bird population and gather enough berries for a month or so of blueberry muffin indulgence. Pat is currently fortunate enough to live just a short hop away from a pick-you-own blueberry farm and can OD in season and lay away a good supply of frozen berries for leaner times of year. When we are not making blueberry muffins or pancakes, we usually put our supply of the fruit into this simple, not-too-sweet cake. Yogurt gives it a wonderfully moist texture and excellent keeping quality. The addition of cardamom is a culinary nod to the Swedish forebears of Bonnie's husband.

Preheat the oven to 350° F. Line the bottom of a 9-inch round baking pan or springform pan, lightly coated with cooking spray, with a round of wax paper cut to fit. Into a bowl sift together the flour, baking powder, baking soda, cardamom, and salt. In a large bowl with a mixer cream together the butter and sugar until the mixture is light and well combined. In a bowl beat the eggs with the yogurt, vanilla, and rind. Add the flour mixture and the egg mixture alternately to the butter mixture, a third at a time, beating lightly after each addition, and fold in the blueberries, dusted with flour. Pour the batter into the baking pan, sprinkle the top with cardamom sugar, and bake the cake for 45 minute, or until a tester inserted in the center comes out clean. Let the cake cool in the pan on a rack for 15 minutes, turn it out onto the rack, and peel off the wax paper. Serve the cake warm, at room temperature, or chilled. Serves 6 to 8.

1¾ cups flour, plus extra for dusting

1 teaspoon baking powder

½ teaspoon baking soda

1 teaspoon ground cardamom

½ teaspoon salt

⅓ cup butter (about 5 tablespoons), softened

¼ cup sugar

2 eggs

an 8-ounce carton vanilla yogurt (or a 6-ounce carton plus ¼ cup milk)

1 teaspoon vanilla

1 teaspoon grated lemon rind

1¼ cups fresh blueberries

2 tablespoons cardamom sugar or cinnamon sugar (adjacent page)

P&B's Hints: Plain vanilla yogurt is fine, but try banana cream, coconut cream, or lemon flavors for variety. Banana is particularly good. The cake is great for tea or breakfast too. For a fancier dessert, add a scoop of ice cream on top along with a drizzling of lemon dessert sauce (page 173).

NECTARINE ALMOND CAKE

1 cup flour

¼ cup yellow cornmeal

1 teaspoon baking powder

½ teaspoon baking soda

¼ teaspoon salt

¾ cup sugar

2 eggs

½ cup milk

¼ cup sour cream

2 teaspoons apricot brandy (or orange juice)

½ teaspoon almond extract

5 tablespoons butter, melted

2 nectarines (one chopped, one thinly sliced) or 3 pluots (1½ chopped, 1½ thinly sliced)

1 tablespoon sliced almonds tossed with 1 tablespoon melted butter

1 teaspoon cinnamon sugar (page 174) for topping

Each summer we looked forward to Grandma's peach cake, crunchy with cornmeal and sliced almonds. Cooling ourselves with large leaf-shaped, split-reed fans and sweet iced tea floating with fresh mint, we'd sit on Grandma's porch glider pretending to be elegant ladies, while devouring slice after slice of this delicious cake. Although we still will use peaches when local ones are in season, nectarines have become the fruit of choice as they are more dependably available and shelf-worthy. Recently, as pluots (a plum/apricot cross) have become more common in the markets, we have experimented with them and found them a good alternative as well.

Preheat the oven to 350° F. Into a bowl sift together the flour, cornmeal, baking powder, baking soda, and salt. In a large bowl beat together the sugar, eggs, milk, sour cream, brandy, and almond extract and gradually beat in the flour mixture until the batter is well combined. Stir in the melted butter and chopped nectarines. Pour the batter into a 9-inch round baking pan (springform if you have it), lightly coated with cooking spray, and top it with the nectarine slices. Scatter the almonds evenly over the mixture, sprinkle the top with the cinnamon sugar or plain sugar, and bake the cake for 45 minutes, or until the top is springy to the touch, the sides pull away slightly from the edge of the pan, and the almonds are crisp and golden. Serves 6 to 8.

P&B's Hints: Although this won't be difficult, try to eat this cake while it is still warm and fresh; the almonds tend to get soggy if the cake sits around, covered, for more than a day. We won't go so far as to say that it will make the cake really much healthier, but the recipe works just fine made with low-fat milk and sour cream.

MIXED BERRY TURNOVERS

Grandma and Mother regularly baked pies and tarts, and Grandma's ultra-flaky lard-based pie crust was to die for in terms of taste and texture (not to mention cholesterol content). These days we rarely have time to turn out pies with a homemade crust. However, thanks to the convenience of store-bought frozen puff pastry—reminiscent of Grandma's pie crust, yet lard-free—these quick-fix little turnovers satisfy a craving for the pastries of our childhood. Feel free to vary the choice of fruits and jam base to suit your taste. We keep a supply of these ready in the freezer with a quart of ice cream or frozen yogurt for an easy family or company dessert.

½ cup seedless raspberry jam

1 teaspoon grated lemon rind

1 teaspoon honey

a 17-ounce package frozen puff pastry, thawed

2 cups mixed blueberries, raspberries, and chopped strawberries

1 egg yolk combined with 2 teaspoons water

granulated sugar for sprinkling

ice cream or frozen yogurt as an accompaniment

In a small bowl combine the jam, rind, and honey. On a lightly floured surface roll half the dough into a 12-inch square and cut the square into 4 equal squares. Spread each square to within ¾ inch of the edges with about 1 tablespoon of the jam and arrange ¼ cup of the fruit mixture on one half of the dough of each square, leaving the edges uncovered. Moisten the edges of each square with water and fold the untopped halves of the dough over the fruit, forming rectangular-shaped turnovers. Seal the edges by pressing them together with the tines of a fork, brush the tops of the turnovers with some of the yolk mixture, and sprinkle them with sugar. Make three small diagonal slits in the top of each turnover to allow moisture to escape during baking and chill the turnovers for 20 minutes, or until they are firm. (The turnovers may be frozen at this point.) Make turnovers with the remaining ingredients in the same manner. Bake the turnovers on a baking sheet, lined with foil that has been lightly coated with cooking spray, in a preheated 375° F. oven for 20 minutes, or until they are puffed and golden (some jam may bubble out, but not to worry). Frozen turnovers can be baked directly from the freezer and will take slightly longer to cook. Serve the turnovers warm or at room temperature with ice cream or frozen yogurt. Makes 8 turnovers.

FROZEN KEY LIME PIE WITH PECAN CRUST

1¾ cups pecans, finely ground and combined with ¼ cup graham cracker crumbs

¼ cup lightly packed light brown sugar

3 tablespoons butter, melted

3 eggs, yolks and whites separated

2 limes, rind grated and juice squeezed

1 cup heavy cream

Ooops...also add
½ cup white sugar
(whisk it together with the yolks, lime juice, and rind)

Although Grandma used nuts a lot in her pastries, cakes, and cookies, we can't remember her ever having used them for pie crust. Her pie crusts were always made with lard. Mindful of Daddy's cholesterol, Mother branched out into graham cracker crusts for her pies, as well as for bar cookies and cheesecake. We have married the graham cracker crust tradition with nuts and make various combinations of the two for some of our own desserts, especially this key lime pie. It is a great dessert to have in the freezer, made ahead for a party or ready to serve unexpected company.

In a bowl combine the pecan mixture, brown sugar, and butter. Press the mixture into the bottom and up the sides of a 9-inch pie pan, lightly coated with cooking spray, and chill it, loosely covered, for 20 minutes. Preheat the oven to 350° F. Bake the pie shell for 15 minutes, or until it is lightly browned, and let it cool in the pan on a rack. In a small nonreactive saucepan whisk together the yolks, lime juice, and rind and cook the mixture over moderately low heat, stirring, until it is thickened. Transfer the mixture to a large bowl and let it cool slightly. In separate bowls beat the egg whites until they hold stiff peaks and beat the cream until it holds stiff peaks. Stir a third of the whites into the lime mixture to lighten it, then gently but thoroughly fold in the remaining whites followed by the whipped cream. Pour the mixture into the pie shell, smoothing it, and freeze the pie, covered with plastic wrap, until it is solid. Let the pie soften slightly just before serving. Serves 8 to 10.

P&B's Hints: For extra richness eliminate the graham cracker crumbs from the crust and use a total of 2 cups ground pecans. Alternatively, although it won't be nearly as unctuous, if you are really pressed, you can simply use a store-bought graham cracker crust with this filling. Or, if you want to cut back on a few calories and fat grams, serve the filling, crustless, in individual ramekins as frozen soufflés.

CHOCOLATE BOURBON PECAN PIE

The closest Grandma came to making a traditional Southern-style pecan pie was something called shoofly pie, a homier, simpler dessert thought to be of Pennsylvania Dutch origin. It had a similar sticky-sweet filling but with molasses as the predominant flavor, plus a streusel-like topping. As soon as we discovered Southern pecan pie, its luscious decadence lured us away from the Pennsylvania Dutch simplicity. We have since doctored the basic pecan pie further, first with bourbon and then with chocolate.

Preheat the oven to 375° F. Prick the pie shell all over with a fork, line it with wax paper, and fill the paper with dried beans, rice, or pie weights. Bake the shell for 15 minutes, remove the wax paper and beans, and bake the shell for 15 minutes more, or until it is lightly browned. Let the shell cool in the pan on a rack while you make the filling. Reduce the oven to 350° F. In a large microwaveable bowl melt the butter and chocolate together in the microwave, stirring occasionally, and stir in the corn syrup. In another bowl beat together the eggs, sugar, bourbon, and vanilla and stir the mixture into the chocolate mixture. Pour the mixture into the pie shell, scatter the pecans evenly on the top, and bake the pie for 45 minutes, or until the filling is set in the center. (If the crust starts to become too dark, cover it a strip of foil.) Let the pie cool in the pan on a rack. Serves 8 to 10.

a 9-inch homemade or store-bought pie crust

4 tablespoons butter

4 ounces semisweet chocolate, broken in pieces

¾ cup light corn syrup

3 eggs

⅓ cup lightly packed dark brown sugar

2 tablespoons bourbon or dark rum

1 teaspoon vanilla

1½ cups coarsely chopped pecans

PUDDING

Before the days of cavernous refrigerators, the limited space on the chilly shelves of one's icebox was reserved for important perishables. Everyday desserts that could be served warm from the oven or at room temperature were understandably popular. (Anyone remember those old pie safes that turn up occasionally in antiques shops?) Without the year-round availability of fresh fruit that we enjoy today, desserts based on pantry staples—eggs, milk, dried fruits, and flavor extracts—ranked high on the list of offerings in our house. Cakes, pies, and puddings were a huge part of our family recipe file, with puddings being the dessert we saw most often. All that milk and egg goodness was irresistible to a mother trying to compete with Twinkies and the like. Over the years we have, in moments of weakness (or desperation), tried packaged pudding mixes, instant pudding concoctions, and even those prepared puddings in their individual plastic cups. All are OK in their place—but that place does not happen to be in our kitchens. Nothing can compare with the flavor and consistency of a homemade pudding or custard. Most take only a few minutes longer to make than the packaged mixes, but the final products are vastly superior in taste, variety, and nutritional value.

DESSERT BREAD PUDDING

Bread pudding had the virtue of being made quickly with everyday staples and, like stuffing or French toast, was a thrifty way to make use of bread that was past its prime for sandwiches. To us, bread pudding has always been the ultimate in dessert comfort food. This recipe is essentially the basic one handed down from Grandma. We have however lightened it with fat-free dairy and over the years incorporated all manner of flavorful additions and substitutions, a number of which are given below in the Hints.

Preheat oven to 350° F. Spread the bread cubes in a 1½- to 2-quart baking dish, lightly coated with cooking spray. In a bowl beat together the half-and-half, eggs, cornstarch, sugar, vanilla, cinnamon, and nutmeg. Gently pour the mixture over the bread cubes and let the mixture stand for a few minutes to allow the bread to absorb some of the liquid. Bake the pudding for 1 hour, or until it is puffed and springy in the center. Serves 6.

3 cups bread cubes, cut from slightly stale, firm-textured white bread

2½ cups fat-free half-and-half

3 eggs

1 teaspoon cornstarch

⅓ cup sugar

1 teaspoon vanilla

½ teaspoon cinnamon (optional—eliminate if not compatible with other additions)

¼ teaspoon nutmeg (optional—eliminate if not compatible with other additions)

P&B's Hints: Replace part of the half-and-half with eggnog, fruit nectar, maple syrup, applesauce, fruit yogurt, or fruit baby food. Use cubed pound cake instead of bread. Also try adding ¼ cup finely chopped dried fruits such as prunes, apricots, or cranberries, softened in boiling water and drained well; ¼ cup marmalade or fruit preserves; ¼ cup well drained crushed pineapple; ½ to 1 teaspoon rum extract; or the grated rind of ½ lemon or orange. For a special pudding with minimal effort, use cinnamon swirl or cinnamon-raisin bread. For a Scandinavian treat use corn bread, add ½ cup golden raisins, and replace the cinnamon and nutmeg with 1 teaspoon ground cardamom.

CHOCOLATE MINT PUDDING CAKE

1 cup flour

¾ cup unsweetened cocoa powder

½ cup white sugar

2 teaspoons baking powder

½ teaspoon cinnamon

½ cup low-fat milk

3 tablespoons canola oil

1 teaspoon vanilla

½ cup light packed brown sugar

¼ cup semisweet chocolate chips, finely chopped in a food processor

¼ teaspoon mint extract, or more if you really like a minty flavor

whipped cream, ice cream, or frozen yogurt as an accompaniment if desired

Among the custardy desserts that appeared regularly in our house, chocolate pudding cake reigned supreme. We loved it not just because it was chocolate but also because it was a delicious combination of gooey and cake-y. Daddy loved it simply because it was dessert. Mother loved it because she generally made it with a packaged mix (without letting Grandma in on this little secret) and thus it was snap to put together, could be made ahead, and was an inexpensive way to please everyone in the family. We were fascinated by the magic of the preparation (we still are): how liquid poured on top of the batter mixture ended up as pudding under a layer of cake after the baking. We now make a slightly more grown-up version of that pudding cake, with a hint of mint.

Preheat the oven to 350° F. In a bowl combine the flour, ½ cup of the cocoa powder, the white sugar, baking powder, and cinnamon, stir in the milk, canola oil, and vanilla, and spread the batter in an 8-inch-square nonstick baking pan. In a small dish combine the remaining ¼ cup cocoa powder, the brown sugar, and chocolate chips and sprinkle the mixture over the batter. In a microwaveable bowl bring 1¾ cups water to a boil, add the mint extract, and slowly and carefully pour the boiling water mixture evenly over the batter in the pan but do not stir. Bake the pudding cake for 30 minutes, or until the cake layer that has risen to the top is lightly springy and pulling away from the sides of the pan slightly. Let the pudding cake cool in the pan on a rack for at least 10 minutes, then spoon it into dessert bowls or coupes and top each serving with whipped cream if desired. Serves 6 to 8.

182

EXTRA-QUICK TAPIOCA PUDDING

Tapioca pudding, long out of fashion as boring and dowdy, is enjoying a renaissance. We've taken a simple dessert staple of our childhood and added an array of fruits and flavorings (see below) to create a homey comfort food with contemporary taste appeal. Though not quite as light and luxurious as the old-fashioned tapioca into which Grandma incorporated stiffly beaten egg whites, this version is faster and you have only a measuring cup and one pan to wash.

½ cup sugar

3½ tablespoons quick-cooking tapioca

2 cups milk

1 egg

a pinch of salt

1 teaspoon vanilla

In a saucepan whisk together all the ingredients except the vanilla and bring the mixture to a boil over moderately high heat, stirring occasionally. Reduce the heat to moderately low and cook the mixture, stirring occasionally, for 10 minutes, or until it is thickened. Remove the pan from the heat and stir in the vanilla. Serve the tapioca warm or chilled. Serves 4.

SOME SUGGESTED ADDITIONS

- the grated rind of ½ orange and 1 teaspoon orange-flavored liqueur
- 1 teaspoon ground ginger and ¼ cup minced crystallized ginger
- ½ teaspoon rum extract and ½ teaspoon grated nutmeg
- ½ cup golden raisins
- 1 teaspoon ground cardamom and ¼ cup minced apple
- 2 tablespoons maple syrup or 1½ teaspoons maple extract
- 1 tablespoon instant coffee dissolved in 1 tablespoon hot water
- 1 tablespoon unsweetened cocoa powder
- ½ teaspoon rosewater and ¼ cup ground pistachio nuts (sprinkled on top)
- ⅓ cup toasted shredded coconut (sprinkled on top)
- fresh berries or chopped fresh fruit such as peaches, apricots, or kiwis to taste

INDIAN-STYLE RICE PUDDING

1¾ cups lite coconut milk

2 cups fat-free half-and-half or whole milk

3 tablespoons sugar

½ cup basmati or other long-grain rice

½ teaspoon ground cardamom

1-inch cinnamon stick

¼ cup golden raisins

½ teaspoon rose water or almond extract

¼ cup sliced blanched almonds, lightly toasted, or chopped pistachios

Grandma or Mother's rice pudding landed on our dinner table frequently. Basically a mixture of rice, milk, and sugar with cinnamon or nutmeg, it could be prepared ahead, then simmered slowly on the stove, and served warm for dinner. Although we go for a little more flavor excitement in our desserts these days, we still love the make-ahead quality and homey comfort of rice pudding. Inspired by Indian restaurant dining, we now often end a spicy meal with a pudding that combines Grandma's dessert and the Indian classic kheer. Along with the cardamom, the rose water really makes this dessert and is worth seeking out in the international foods section of the supermarket or a specialty foods shop.

In a heavy saucepan bring the coconut milk and half-and-half to a boil over moderate heat, stirring. Stir in the sugar, rice, cardamom, and cinnamon stick and simmer the mixture, stirring occasionally, for 20 minutes, or until it is thickened and the rice is just cooked through but still al dente. Discard the cinnamon stick and stir in the raisins and rose water. Serve the pudding warm or chilled, topped with the almonds. Serves 4 to 6.

P&B's Hints: Any combination of low-fat or full-fat dairy products works fine here, as does medium-grain rice if you prefer its texture. We also occasionally substitute chopped dried apricots for the raisins and also stir in a tablespoon or two of unsweetened flaked coconut.

MOCHA CRÈME BRULÉE

Among the kitchen equipment we inherited from Grandma and Mother was an inordinate number of custard cups, molds, and steamers, leaving little doubt as to what type of dessert appeared most frequently in our house. We haven't seen any reason to break with the family "pudding" tradition. These days, however, the custard gracing our dinner tables is more likely to be some version of crème brulée. Using the best chocolate we can find and adding a hint of coffee, we lavish on this dessert the time and attention of Grandma's made-from-scratch approach, and it has become our current "haute" custard of choice.

Preheat the oven to 350° F. In a baking pan approximately 9 by 13 inches arrange six ¾-cup ramekins. In a saucepan melt the chocolate over low heat, stirring, and whisk in the white sugar. Gradually whisk in the cream and cook the mixture at a bare simmer, stirring, until the chocolate and sugar are completely dissolved and the mixture is smooth. Remove the pan from the heat, stir in the coffee granules, and let the mixture cool, stirring occasionally, for 5 minutes. In a bowl beat the yolks with the cinnamon and vanilla until they are frothy, whisk in the chocolate mixture, a little at a time, and whisk the custard until it is smooth. Divide the custard among the ramekins and set the pan in the oven. Add enough hot water to the pan to reach halfway up the sides of the ramekins and bake the custards for 25 minutes, or until they are just set. Remove the ramekins from the pan, let the custards cool, and chill them, covered, until they are cold or overnight. Sprinkle each custard with 1½ to 2 teaspoons fine granulated sugar and put the custards under a preheated broiler for several minutes, or until the sugar is bubbling and turns a light caramel. Chill the custards for 1 hour, or until they are cold and the topping hardens. Serves 6.

⅓ cup chopped semisweet chocolate or chocolate chips (the better quality of chocolate, the better the custard will be)

¼ cup white sugar

2 cups heavy cream

1½ teaspoons instant coffee or espresso granules

4 egg yolks

¼ teaspoon cinnamon

1 teaspoon vanilla

4 tablespoons fine granulated sugar

P&B's Hints: When we make this dessert, it is one of the few times we put aside any thoughts we might have about dieting or healthy eating and just enjoy its pure lusciousness! If you happen to own one of those handy kitchen torches, it makes caramelizing the topping even easier.

STARRY STARRY NIGHTS
Cocoa & Cookies

After the experiences of World War II, America was relieved but also cold-war wary. Having learned from Pearl Harbor, "the powers that be" created civilian teams to man strategically positioned observation posts, tracking and reporting all passing aircraft. As a veteran, our father did his part and took his turn. One night a month he packed up his binoculars and reported for duty—to a wooden tower, high on a barren local hill. He always said the four-hour shift went much faster when we went along, so Mother would fill a thermos with hot chocolate, put some cookies in a small tin box (that to this day still serves in the same capacity) and send us off to what we thought of as a special tree house. Probably not much taller than an old telephone pole, to us the structure rivaled the Empire State Building in stature. With 360° decking, it provided a dazzling panorama of open fields and tree-trimmed horizons, eerie moonlit expanses so enticingly different from our daily milieu of closely clustered houses and neatly mowed lawns. We felt as though we had journeyed to some faraway planet. We'll never forget watching young foxes romping beneath our perch, listening to whippoorwills calling out to all who would listen, and, most of all, on one magical evening, discovering that Bambi was real! Nights spent at the observation post are a special childhood memory. We learned about nature, the stars, duty, and patriotism—and we learned about our father.

MAKE-AHEAD MAPLE NUT COOKIES

Our after-school snack invariably included an apple and milk, plus home-made cookies. These tended to favor the healthy side of the cookie kingdom, generally an oatmeal clone dotted with fruit such as raisins, pineapple, or dried apricots. They were good—don't get us wrong—but they never quite matched up to the thin, rich, extra-buttery nut cookies that Grandma always had on hand tucked away in a large metal tin decorated with a Dickens-esque holiday scene. Almost every cook of Grandma and Mother's generation had a favorite refrigerator cookie recipe in her repertoire, and we've reworked our basic family recipe to create a dough that can be adapted to anyone's taste, keeps well in the refrigerator, and freezes too. With a log of this dough on hand, cookies to rival Grandma's are quick and easy to produce for a snack attack or last-minute dessert—worth the effort because they taste SO much better than their supermarket counterparts.

1¾ cups flour

½ teaspoon baking soda

½ teaspoon salt

a pinch of nutmeg

1 stick (½ cup) butter, softened

1 cup lightly packed brown sugar

1 egg

1 teaspoon vanilla

1½ teaspoons maple extract

½ cup finely chopped walnuts

Into a bowl sift together the flour, baking soda, salt, and nutmeg. In a larger bowl with a mixer cream together well the butter and sugar and beat in the egg, vanilla, and maple extract. Gradually beat in the flour mixture until the dough is well combined. Stir in the walnuts and chill the dough, covered, for about 15 minutes, or until it is firm enough to shape easily. Shape the dough into two logs, 1½ to 1¾ inches in diameter, and chill the logs, wrapped in wax paper or plastic wrap, for at least 1 hour and up to several days. (The dough can also be frozen, well wrapped, at this point.) Preheat the oven to 375° F. With a finely serrated knife, cut ⅛-inch-thick slices from the logs and set them about 1 inch apart on baking sheets that are nonstick or lightly coated with cooking spray. Bake the cookies for 10 minutes, or until they are lightly browned, transfer them to a rack, and let them cool completely. Store the cookies in an airtight container. Makes about 48 cookies.

P&B's Hints: We often substitute pecans, pistachios, almonds, or pine nuts for the walnuts. Grated orange rind works nicely in place of the maple extract, as does 1 teaspoon cinnamon. If baking frozen cookie dough, let the dough thaw in the refrigerator until it is softened just enough to slice. We have found that a serrated knife works best for the slicing.

CINNAMON TORTILLA CRISPS

4 tablespoons sugar

1¼ teaspoons cinnamon

¼ teaspoon nutmeg

a pinch of salt

6 flour tortillas (6-inch), quartered into wedges

3 tablespoons butter, melted with ¼ teaspoon vanilla

Grandma's extensive cookie repertoire included a series of light and elegant crisps such as tricky-to-make lace cookies and tuiles, both of which had to be hand-curled quickly while still hot on the baking sheet. We long ago gave up on these labor-intensive, humidity-sensitive delicacies, searching instead for some comparable but easier alternative. After much experimentation, we came up with this quick Tex-Mex cookie-like crisp, which is made with store-bought tortillas.

Preheat the oven to 400° F. In a small bowl combine well the sugar, cinnamon, nutmeg, and salt. In a large bowl toss the tortilla wedges with the butter mixture until they are well coated. Arrange the tortilla wedges in one layer on a large baking sheet (about 12 by 18 inches), lined with foil, sprinkle them on both sides with the sugar mixture, and bake them for 10 minutes, or until they are golden brown and start to crisp. Let the wedges cool on a rack (they will become crisper as they cool). Makes 24 crisps.

P&B's Hints: If you have a saltshaker with large-ish holes, put the cinnamon-sugar mixture in it and you'll find that the sprinkling is easier and the mixture more evenly disbursed.

BASIC DESSERT BARS

Both Grandma and Mother's cookie repetoires included date bars, and in grade school those sweets were one of the things that made for a "good lunch box day," trumping our friends' store-bought Fig Newtons. Dates are a less common baking ingredient these days, and the bars, once a bake sale staple, have become—pardon the pun—rather dated. Plus, the term "date bar" these days conjures up far racier images than would have entered Grandma's head. We still make the crust from our basic family recipe but have topped it with a variety of different fillings to suit our mood and the occasion. Some of our favorite combinations are listed below.

1½ cups flour

1 cup quick-cooking oats

¾ cup lightly packed brown sugar

½ cup finely chopped walnuts

1½ teaspoons baking soda

1½ sticks (¾ cup) cold butter

Preheat the oven to 350° F. In a bowl combine well the flour, oats, sugar, walnuts, and baking soda. Add the butter, cut into bits, and incorporate it, rubbing the mixture together with your fingers until it is well combined and crumbly. Press slightly more than half of the mixture into a nonstick 9-inch-square baking pan, tamping it down firmly and making a slightly higher rim around the edges. Spread the desired filling mixture (see below) evenly onto but not quite to the edges of the crust in the pan. Sprinkle the remaining crust mixture evenly over the filling, pat it down gently, and bake the mixture for 30 minutes, or until the top is lightly browned. Let the mixture cool completely in the pan on a rack and cut it into small or large bars. Makes thirty-six 1½-inch bars or sixteen 2¼-inch bars.

DATE BAR FILLING: In a small saucepan combine 8 ounces finely chopped pitted dates with ½ cup sugar and 1 tablespoon flour. Add 1 teaspoon lemon juice and 1 cup water, bring the liquid to boil over moderately high heat, stirring often, and simmer the mixture, stirring occasionally, until it is thickened and the dates are very soft. Let the mixture cool for 10 minutes and use as filling in the basic dessert bar recipe.

MINCEMEAT BAR FILLING: (Great for Thanksgiving) Use 2 cups of prepared mincemeat, drained slightly if very watery, as filling in the basic dessert bar recipe.

ALTERNATIVE FILLINGS: Some additional filling options include about 2 cups thick apple butter, apricot preserves, fig jam, puréed cooked prunes, quince paste, or canned whole berry cranberry sauce combined with 1 tablespoon each grated orange rind and Grand Marnier.

RASPBERRY LINZER BARS

FOR THE FILLING:
1 tablespoon lemon juice

¼ teaspoon grated lemon rind

¾ cup raspberry preserves

FOR THE DOUGH:
1¾ cups flour

¼ cup finely ground hazelnuts

¼ teaspoon ground cloves

¼ teaspoon salt

1 stick (½ cup) butter, softened

½ cup lightly packed light brown sugar

1 egg yolk

¼ teaspoon almond extract

FOR THE MERINGUE:
1 egg white

2 tablespoons white sugar

¾ cup finely chopped hazelnuts

First, Grandpa had to crack and shell the tough little hazelnuts—a labor of love and quid pro quo for getting one of his favorite desserts. And then, there had to be some homemade raspberry preserves on hand as well before Grandma could make her lovely lattice-topped, sugar-dusted Linzer torte. In our lazy hands, that luscious torte has mutated into these simpler bar cookies. We use store-bought shelled and skinned hazelnuts and raspberry jam (seeded or seedless) and replace the fussy latticework with a thin layer of crunchy, nutty meringue. We think even Grandma would agree that our adaptation is a pretty good trade off in terms of time and effort.

Preheat the oven to 350° F. Make the filling: In a small bowl stir the lemon juice and rind into the preserves. Make the dough: In another small bowl stir together the flour, ground hazelnuts, cloves, and salt. In a larger bowl with a mixer cream together well the butter and brown sugar, then beat in the yolk and almond extract. Gradually add the flour mixture, beating until the dough is well combined and crumbly. Pat the dough into a 9- by 13-inch baking pan, well coated with cooking spray, and bake it for 15 minutes. When the dough is about ready to come out of the oven, make the meringue: In a bowl beat the egg white until it is foamy, beat in the white sugar, and beat the meringue until it forms soft peaks. Remove the dough from the oven and spread it with the preserves. Drop spoonfuls of the meringue onto the preserves and with a spatula spread the meringue gently over the preserves. Sprinkle the chopped nuts evenly on top and bake the mixture for 25 minutes. Let the mixture cool in the pan on a rack for 30 minutes, transfer it to a cutting board, and trim the edges if desired (eat the trimmings). Cut the mixture into bars and let the bars cool completely before storing in an airtight container for up to a week. Makes 32 bars, about 2 by 1½ inches.

P&B's Hints: If you want to freeze the bars, cut the cooked mixture into two 9- by 6½-inch chunks, let them cool completely, and wrap them up that way, to be cut into bars after they are thawed. An easy way to obtain both ground and chopped hazelnuts is to pour about 2 cups whole nuts into the food processor. Pulse repeatedly until the bowl is filled with a combination of ground and chopped nuts. Pour this mixture into a coarse strainer and shake out the ground nuts into a bowl. Save the chopped nuts separately.

NUTTY COCONUT LEMON TRIANGLES

Over the years the basic lemon bars that Grandma and Mother made on a regular basis have been tweaked by us in every imaginable way, with this Caribbean-accented version being a favorite. We love bar cookies because they can be made ahead and they serve well as that small bite of sweetness we crave after dinner in place of a real dessert. Plus, they transport well—perfect for lunch boxes, picnics, snacks, and those occasions when you might be called upon to contribute a sweet.

Preheat the oven to 275° F. Make the crust: In a food processor pulse together the flour, brown sugar, and butter until the mixture resembles coarse meal and press it into a 9- by 13-inch baking pan, either nonstick or lightly coated with cooking spray. Bake the crust for 15 minutes and let it cool in the pan on a rack while you make the topping. Raise the oven temperature to 350° F. Make the topping: In a large bowl combine the coconut, brown sugar, pecans, flour, baking powder, and salt. In a small bowl beat together well the eggs, vanilla, and rind and stir the mixture into the coconut mixture. Spread the topping over the crust almost to the edges and bake the mixture for 20 minutes, or until it is well puffed and crisp on top. Let the bar mixture cool in the pan on a rack for 5 minutes. While the bar mixture is cooling make the glaze: In a small bowl beat together the confectioners' sugar, lemon juice, and rind until the mixture is smooth and drizzle or spread it over the bar mixture. Trim off the ragged edges of the bar mixture if desired for a more attractive presentation (eat the trimmings), quarter the mixture both lengthwise and crosswise, and then cut each piece into 2 triangles. Makes 32 bar cookies.

FOR THE CRUST:
1½ cups flour

½ cup lightly packed brown sugar

1 stick (½ cup) butter, cut into bits

FOR THE TOPPING:
1¾ cups flaked sweetened coconut

1 cup lightly packed brown sugar

¾ cup finely chopped pecans

3 tablespoons flour

½ teaspoon baking powder

¼ teaspoon salt

3 eggs

1 teaspoon vanilla

1 teaspoon grated lemon rind

FOR THE GLAZE:
1¼ cups sifted confectioners' sugar

2 tablespoons plus 1 teaspoon lemon juice

1 teaspoon grated lemon rind

CHOCOLATE TASSIES

FOR THE CRUST:
1 stick (½ cup) butter, softened

4 ounces cream cheese, softened

1 cup flour

2 tablespoons cocoa powder

½ teaspoon baking powder

2 tablespoons brown sugar

2 tablespoons finely ground walnuts

1 tablespoon milk

FOR THE FILLING:
6 ounces semisweet chocolate or chocolate chips (about 1 cup)

1 tablespoon butter

1 tablespoon milk

1 egg

⅓ cup white sugar

1 teaspoon vanilla

⅓ cup currants

Tassie is an old-fashioned rather prissy-sounding word, conjuring up images of teatime in a formal front parlor. Though its origins could be traced to Russia as a nickname for Natasha, it probably owes its culinary lineage more to the Scottish term for cup. It was a popular sweet in Grandma's era and is still commonly found in many parts of the South, usually with a sticky-sweet pecan filling. Grandma generally favored a pie-style crust with a nut or lemon filling, but, after dinner we (husbands especially) love something chocolate. Thus we created these richly delicious little morsels to satisfy our sweets craving without adding the caloric load of a big dessert. Try to eat just one.

Make the crust: In a bowl cream together the butter and cream cheese. Into a bowl sift together the flour, cocoa, and baking powder. Stir the flour mixture into the butter mixture along with the brown sugar, walnuts, and milk, and combine the mixture well. Form the dough into 1-inch balls (about 30 of them) and chill them, well wrapped, for at least an hour or overnight. Make the filling: In a small saucepan heat the chocolate, butter, and milk over moderately low heat, stirring, until the chocolate is melted, and let the mixture cool slightly. In a bowl beat together well the egg, white sugar, and vanilla, and stir in the chocolate mixture and currants. Preheat the oven to 350° F. On a sheet of wax paper with the heel of your hand flatten the balls of dough into 2½-inch rounds. Press the rounds lightly into mini muffin tins about 1¾ inches in diameter so that the top of the dough comes up just slightly above the rim of the muffin tins. Divide the chocolate mixture among the tassie cups, filling them about ¾ full, and bake the tassies for 25 minutes, or until the chocolate mixture is puffed and set. Let the tassies cool in the tins for 5 minutes and gently transfer them to a rack to cool completely. Makes about 30 tassies.

P&B's Hints: To save saucepan cleanup and preserve every last bit of the filling, we melt the chocolate mixture in a heatproof bowl in the microwave and add the other ingredients to it. We also will often add a ½ teaspoon of instant coffee granules for a mocha taste or replace the currants with chopped dried cherries or cranberries (craisins) or toasted coconut.

SUGAR-FROSTED PECANS

Every year sometime during the Christmas holidays we would gather at Grandma's house to watch a performance of the Nutcracker Suite ballet on television. The Sugar Plum Fairy was magical in our minds, and we always equated her with Grandma's sugar-frosted pecans. Almost everyone we know has a family recipe for this popular sweet treat. Ours is pretty straightforward, though we tend to branch out from the original in the flavorings, with orange and maple being the most common departures. We honor Grandma's tradition, however, of whipping up batches of these nuts during the holidays, which—wrapped in little brightly colored cellophane packages—make their way around with us as we visit friends.

4 tablespoons butter

1 cup sugar

1 teaspoon cinnamon

½ teaspoon nutmeg

2 egg whites

¼ teaspoon cream of tartar

1 teaspoon vanilla

½ teaspoon orange extract or maple extract

1 pound pecan halves

Preheat the oven to 325° F. In a 9- by 14-inch baking pan melt the butter, swirling it around to coat the pan. In a small bowl combine the sugar, cinnamon, and nutmeg. In a larger bowl beat the egg whites with the cream of tartar until they hold moderately stiff peaks and fold in the sugar mixture, vanilla, and orange extract. Fold in the pecans, stirring gently until the nuts are well coated with the egg white mixture. Pour the mixture into the pan and bake it, stirring every 10 minutes, for about 30 minutes, or until the nuts are almost dry. Pour the nuts out onto foil, separating any that stick together. Let the nuts cool completely and store them in an airtight container. Makes about 4½ cups.

P&B's Hints: Of late we've been giving these nuts a slightly Scandinavian twist by substituting 2 teaspoons ground cardamom for the cinnamon and orange extract.

BEVERAGES
Afternoon Tea

There were so many reasons we loved visiting with Grandma aside from the fact that she was just a wonderful grandmother. There was her pretty terraced backyard garden. There was the large glider swing on the screened porch. There was the gentle old cocker spaniel. There was the TV (she had one long before we did!). There was always something cooking that smelled delicious. And then there was afternoon tea. Grandma drank a "cuppa" every afternoon, sometimes on the run, but when we came to visit she made more of an occasion of teatime. While Grandpa drank his instant Sanka, Grandma brewed a pot of tea. We watched the process in wonder as she opened the large tin of Hu-Kwa brand Lapsang Souchong, which seemed very exotic with its colorful bird and flower motifs outlined in gold against a black background. This was the only tea Grandma drank, and tea bags were never even a consideration. She deposited spoonfuls of the coarse, curly black tea leaves into the warmed Woods Ware teapot, added furiously boiling water, then let the mixture steep for several minutes. For us she half-filled the large, intricately patterned teacups with warm milk, laid a lacy silver tea strainer across the top of each cup, and poured in a small amount of the strong smoky brew. We then added our desired quota of mini sugar cubes. And, needless to say, tea was accompanied by a big plate of homemade cookies. Though we rarely have time to indulge in anything so gracious as Grandma's afternoon teatime ritual, a tin of Hu-Kwa (a specialty order item these days) is still a staple in our own cupboards.

CHAI (INDIAN SPICED TEA)

1 cup water

1 teaspoon sugar, or to taste

1 clove

a 1-inch piece cinnamon stick

1 cardamom pod, lightly crushed

1 whole allspice, lightly crushed

2 to 3 teaspoons loose black tea

½ cup hot milk

Our present passion for Chai probably originated in all the afternoon teatimes we spent with Grandma and a lingering taste memory of the smoky Lapsang Souchong tea and milk combination she always served us. With the current revival in popularity of this Indian-style tea, you can easily purchase Chai tea bags or mixes or hustle off to the nearest Starbucks for the already brewed-up stuff. We prefer to take the little extra time necessary to make it from scratch, however, because it really does taste better and we know it would please Grandma.

In a small saucepan combine the water, sugar, and spices and bring the mixture to a boil over moderately low heat. Remove the pan from the heat, stir in the tea leaves, and let the mixture steep, covered, for about 5 minutes. Pour the mixture through a fine strainer into a warmed mug or large teacup and stir in the hot milk. Makes 1 serving.

P&B's Hints: We often toss in a slice of fresh or a lump of crystallized ginger, substitute honey for the sugar, or use green tea instead of black.

LEMONADE ICED TEA

Arriving at Grandma's on a summer afternoon, we were usually put to work, mainly pulling garden weeds—a definite downside to the visit. The pride of Grandma's garden was a trellis of large peach-colored Peace roses. Etched indelibly in memory is a picture of our kindly, gentle grandmother murderously squashing any Japanese beetle foolhardy enough to mount an attack on her prized roses. When our chores were done, there was always a big pitcher of iced tea waiting and cookies as well—a definite upside to the visit. Grandma's iced tea included fresh-squeezed lemon juice, home-made sugar syrup, and muddled sprigs of mint to add flavor and fragrance. Mother usually made a streamlined version with canned lemonade. Various styles of iced tea have their passionate devotees, and, while we can respect the different points of view, this remains our favored combination. What follows is hardly a recipe, but it will serve to give the rough proportions that we use for this quick summer refresher.

2 quarts boiling water

6 tea bags (whatever brand or flavor you like)

2 mint tea bags

1 small can frozen lemonade (we favor pink), defrosted

sprigs of mint

In a large heatproof bowl or pitcher steep the tea bags in the boiling water for 10 minutes. Remove the tea bags and chill the tea, covered, until it is cold. Stir in the lemonade to taste. Serve the iced tea in tall glasses with ice and the mint sprigs. Serves 6 to 8.

P&B's Hints: We will occasionally add lime, orange, or tangerine juice to the tea or puréed fresh strawberries. For variety add any variously flavored tea bags that you might like.

SANGRÍA

1 bottle fruity red wine, well chilled

⅓ cup Cointreau or triple sec

¼ cup brandy or dark rum

½ cup orange juice

⅓ cup defrosted frozen lemonade

2 cups chilled ginger ale or club soda, or to taste

superfine granulated sugar to taste

1 orange, cut into ¼-inch slices, seeded, and coarsely chopped

1 small apple, quartered lengthwise, cored, and cut crosswise into thin wedges

a dozen or so seedless red grapes, halved

Summer dinners in our house generally included refreshing iced tea for the adults and, for us children, lemonade, into which was mixed greater amounts of iced tea as we acquired a taste for it. Back then, wine drinking was somehow viewed as being more European than American, and thus the selection of wine and its general availability was relatively limited. Though confirmed wine drinkers these days, when the weather turns warmer, we still enjoy a refreshing glass of lemonade. In light of that, it is only natural perhaps that we have developed a fondness for sangría with its tangy blend of wine and fruit. Like many of our creations, sangría is something we rarely make exactly the same way every time. The following will give you an idea of our general approach to this Spanish-inspired libation. We believe there are no real right or wrong ways to make it—take what you like from this recipe and add your own variations.

In a very large pitcher combine the wine, Cointreau, brandy, orange juice, lemonade, and ginger ale and stir in the sugar to taste. Stir in the orange, apple, and grapes and pour the sangría into wineglasses, being sure to include some of the fruit in each serving. Serves 8 to 10.

P&B's Hints: The flavors will be blended more fully if the entire mixture (minus the ginger ale and sugar) is chilled, covered, for several hours or overnight. Add the ginger ale and sugar just before serving.

LADIES LUNCH PUNCH

To wash down birthday cake or cookies at our childhood parties, Mother would always come up with some tasty blend of fruit juices (lemonade with grape juice was always a hit and almost as good, we thought, as Kool-Aid, which Grandma deemed undrinkable). These days when iced tea seems just a little too boring for a festive luncheon, we tend to revert to the fruit juice habit, with a touch more exoticism in the ingredient mix however. Among our various experiments, this punch has consistently ranked high in the opinion of our guests. It is great as is—or you can add up to three cups each of light rum and apricot brandy or peach schnapps for a more spirited occasion.

In a very large pitcher combine the first five ingredients and chill the mixture, covered, up to one day in advance. Just before serving combine the juice mixture with the soda and add the lime slices. Serve the punch in smaller pitchers or in a punch bowl if desired. Makes about 2 dozen 6-ounce servings.

6 cups (48 ounces) peach/mango juice or a mixture of mango nectar and peach nectar

1½ cups (12 ounces) tamarind nectar

¾ cup (6 ounces) coconut/pineapple juice

2 cups prepared lemonade

1 cup freshly brewed orange spice tea

a 2-liter bottle lemon-lime soda, well chilled

1 lime, halved lengthwise and thinly sliced crosswise

SMOOTHIES

There was no such thing as a "smoothie" in our childhood vocabulary. We routinely consumed a homemade concoction, however, that shared basic elements of that drink, which became a popular juice bar specialty in the 1990s. In her new-fangled blender Mother whirred up a mixture that included a frozen very ripe banana, milk, vanilla, and—horror of horrors for the botulism wary—a raw egg. In later years when yogurt became a supermarket staple it replaced the milk, and a variety of blender smoothies became our on-the-run breakfast of choice. Extensive experimenting has taken us through virtually every fruit in the market, every juice combination, and additions from soy milk to chocolate syrup. In general we have found that a blender makes better smoothies than a food processor as it tends to handle ice cubes and frozen ingredients better. If you long ago traded in your blender for the food processor as many people did, just make sure your ingredients are well chilled. It's hard to go wrong in making a smoothie: Just assemble your choice of fruits or juices and yogurt and keep adding and tasting until you've reached the desired texture and flavor mix. As a jumping-off point, here are a few combos that we enjoy regularly—with no raw egg!

STRAWBERRY BANANA SMOOTHIE: ¾ cup chopped strawberries (chilled or frozen), 1 very ripe banana (chilled or frozen), ½ cup yogurt, ½ cup vanilla soy milk

PEACHES AND CREAM SMOOTHIE: 1½ cups chopped peaches (chilled or frozen), ½ very ripe banana (chilled or frozen), ½ cup peach nectar, ½ cup vanilla yogurt, ½ cup fat-free half-and-half, a pinch of cinnamon

MANGO LASSI: 1½ cups chopped mango (chilled or frozen), ½ cup mango, apricot, or peach nectar, ¾ cup yogurt, ½ cup lite coconut milk, ½ teaspoon vanilla, freshly grated nutmeg to taste

BREAKFAST CAFE LATTE SMOOTHIE: 1 very ripe banana (chilled or frozen), ¾ cup cold strong brewed coffee or espresso, ½ cup fat-free half-and-half, ½ cup vanilla yogurt, 1 teaspoon cocoa powder

ROOT BEER FLOATS

Every night in summer the Good Humor truck would slowly make its jingling way down the tree-shaded street where we lived. Although we claimed we couldn't hear Mother's repeated calls to leave our badminton or croquet game and come inside to clean up for dinner, we had no trouble hearing the truck's tuneful jingle at least three streets away. Our hands-down favorite Good Humors were toasted almond ice cream stick for Pat and orange Creamsicle for Bonnie. Both of these were occasional treats, however, no matter how much we whined. On off nights, Mother would pacify us with homemade root beer floats. Known also in some parts as "brown cows" (though we never called them that), they were simplicity itself: scoops of vanilla ice cream with root beer poured over them and, in our house, a maraschino cherry on top from the supply kept on hand for the adults' pre-dinner Manhattans. We made the floats in tall footed glasses with sloping sides and large round handles, which were specially designated for the purpose, and we each had a favorite color long, slender plastic "iced tea" spoon for mashing the ice cream into the fizzy root beer. The Good Humors held a more exotic lure, but the root beer floats remain the sweeter taste memory.

RECIPE INDEX